When Love Came from the Dark
by Edward Jordan
Gotham Books

book review by Nicole Yurcaba

"*A portrait of a bronze star
That's what you are chiseled to perfection.*"

In this poetry collection, an honest speaker reveals his innermost desires while living in a dark world. Rooted in love and faith, these poems encourage readers to approach life with love and grace. "Everything is Gonna Be Alright" reminds them that one's faith can be the ultimate light in a world filled with evil. In "Your Superman," a devoted speaker reminds a willing audience that sacrificing for others can be a meaningful part of one's purpose. "Please Mend! Please Make Strong Again!" is a unique prayer all its own. Other poems like "Happy Valentine's Day" serve as playful reminders that despite a long journey with someone, each day with that person can be a special gift. These poems bear a distinctive voice. That voice is, at times, intimate and personal. At other times, that voice is philosophical and encouraging.

Part of this collection's charm is that in the poetry everyday experiences and interactions become significant moments. The poems preserve these moments in their own special way. Another facet of these poems is their positive outlook. They encourage one to take difficult situations and transform them into learning experiences. They also remind the reader that finding the positive can be difficult, but if one looks hard enough, they can find it. Many of the poems also remind readers that each experience one has provides its own beneficial lesson. People looking to add a positive influence to their day will appreciate this collection, and those new to the poetry genre will find these poems easy to access and relate to.

When Love Came from the Dark

A POETRY BOOK
COLLECTION

Written by:
Edward Jordan

Gotham Books

30 N Gould St.
Ste. 20820, Sheridan, WY 82801
https://gothambooksinc.com/

Phone: 1 (307) 464-7800

© 2023 *Edward Jordan*. All rights reserved.

No part of this book may be reproduced, stored in a retrieval system, or transmitted by any means without the written permission of the author.

Published by Gotham Books (November 4, 2023)

ISBN: 979-8-88775-724-7 (H)
ISBN: 979-8-88775-585-4 (P)
ISBN: 979-8-88775-723-0 (E)

Because of the dynamic nature of the Internet, any web addresses or links contained in this book may have changed since publication and may no longer be valid.

The views expressed in this work are solely those of the author and do not necessarily reflect the views of the publisher, and the publisher hereby disclaims any responsibility for them.

TABLE OF CONTENTS

Foreword	xiv
Dedication	xv
Reader's Reviews	xvi
You're my World	1
Witchcraft and Magic.... It's Extraordinary	2
The Shield of your Love	3
Everything is Gonna be Alright	4
In Hell on Earth	6
Heart of Gold	8
A Little Wonder	9
Loving You	10
In Loving Memory of a Superman... In the eyes of my Heart a Hero! To a Child... A Giant!	11
I Chose Death	12
Happy Valentine's Day	13
Come Listen to my Heart	14
Society Girl	15
When I Dream	16
You're Truly an Angel	17
Just Tell Me	18
A Beautiful Sunrise	19
How I Fell for You	20
I Ask Not	21
Happy Anniversary	22
Just Trying to say Thanks	23
A Sunrise	24
I Speak Honestly	26

It's Forever	28
On My Street	29
With Every Breath	30
Imprisoned in Life	31
My Peace.... My World!	32
If My Heart Could Speak	33
Happy Birthday	34
Of You!... I Need More	35
I'm Still Standing	36
Mistakes.... I Make	37
Indeed, I Will Honor You	38
What Love Can Do	40
In You... I Believe	42
Forever With You	44
Forever Yours	46
I Promise	47
Within My Reach	49
The Journey	50
Man... I Am	52
Those He Bless	53
Just Wanna Make You Mine	54
Change Your Mind	56
Just Take a Chance	58
Twinkling Star	59
It's Hell	61
My Heart Screams	62
A Wishful Heart	64
A Life Long Mission	66

Dance Wit' Cha	67
I'll Never Love Again	68
I'm Dedicated	69
Until We Meet Again	70
My Balance	71
Believe In Us.... I Do!	72
Still the Same	74
When Evil Rose	75
My Heaven	77
My Tomorrow	78
A Silly Girl	79
Never Wanted You to Go	81
Missing You	83
I Thank You	84
I Vow	85
The Breath of Me	86
The Best Part	87
A Winter Season	88
It's Time for Me... To Face My Fears	89
I Dream of a Tomorrow	91
You're A Flame	93
I Wish Every Day... Could Be Another Yesterday	95
The Essence of My Heart's Pleasure	97
An Impeccable Prize	99
No Lies	100
Happy Valentine's Day But it's no fairy tale...	101
Just One!	102
If Only Tomorrow Would Come	103

Forever Mine	105
Happy Valentine's Day	106
Happy Mother's Day	107
High School	108
If Only I Had a Chance	110
You're The Warrior	111
Resurrected	112
A Bachelor No More	114
An Angel Came... When I Called His Name	115
Summertime	116
Thinking of You	118
My Peace My World	119
In Just a Day a Lifetime I Live	120
You're the Reason!	122
Giving Thanks!	123
Bright Nights... Await me!	124
Simply Wonderful	125
My Only Wish	126
A Lonely Grave	127
I Really Miss You (Remix)	128
You Love Me	129
Nothing Left	130
This Song's for You	131
The World is Hooked on You	132
Heart to Heart	133
My Simple Thanks	134
Another Bad Dream... That's All!	135
Really Missing You	136

Because of You!	137
It's Insane	138
Blessed	140
Chocolate	141
Dream with Me	142
You're Truly Amazing	144
Happy Valentine's Day – Happy Anniversary	145
Mistakes, Mistakes	147
Thuggin' in the Big House	149
In the Ghetto Nothing was Ever Promised	151
Let me Love You	152
Being Fast	153
Old Fashion Cowboy	154
Moments with You	156
Happy Birthday	158
Yours	159
Though Imprisoned 'You Made Me Whole'	160
Just Because	162
No Hold it!	163
My One Desire	165
Loving You	166
Don't Ever Leave	167
My Little Friend	169
Moments	170
Missing You	171
Always There	172
Life Would Be Complete	173
Jazz	175

Happy Birthday	177
Another Wonder	178
Good Girl vs. Bad Boy	180
The Weekend	182
Let Me Shake You Down!	183
I'm Saying Please...	185
Hooked on You	187
When the Storm Comes...	188
Pretty Girl I Need your Attention	189
I Wonder	190
My Kind of Rain	191
Happy Valentine's Day	192
My Only Drug	193
This Ain't No Joke	194
On Your Leash	195
The Peace Within My Soul	197
Never the Reason	198
Sounds Sort of Silly	199
Merry Christmas from the Home of my Heart	200
On this Earth for Sure	201
An Angel	202
When we Met!	203
I Reach for You	205
Happy Mother's Day	206
A Woman's Love	207
Candy I Miss (Remix)	208
Black Woman	209
Jingle Bells! Jingle Bells!	210

Happy Valentine's Day	211
Tears Tears	212
Because You're Special!	213
It Comes Much to Slow	215
Thank You	216
Happy Valentine's Day My Dear	217
The Things I See	218
No Sympathy	219
You're the Music in my World	220
Enslaved	222
Dear Lord	223
For Love's Sake	224
When I'm Alone	225
World to Me	226
Your Superman	227
Thinking of You	229
Thinking of You (Part II)	230
Broken Wings Broken Dreams	231
Never Without	232
Could it be Magic	233
Thinking of You (Part III)	234
Happy Valentine's Day	235
Touched by Angel	236
Please Mend! Please Make Strong Again	237
A Happy Camper	239
The Magic Wand	240
Thinking of You (Part IV)	241
Hooked on You	242

International Husbands' Association in Recognition of Outstanding Achievements... Proudly Presents the 2022 Wife of the Year Award to: 243

We Celebrate his Coming 244

You're Beautiful 246

Forever Thankful 247

I am Lost 248

I Like You 249

I Miss You 250

I Wish I Didn't have to Miss You 251

It's All True 252

Loving your Recipe 253

My Primary 254

My Wish 255

You're not Alone 256

Erase all of my Pains 257

About the Author 258

FOREWORD

I have often wondered about my purpose in life. I have often wondered about how to contribute. Something positive to another person's life. I think about an ingredient that can be added to the recipe that makes mankind's happiness brighter. I have forever hoped before my final call to possess the magic wand that would allow me to touch the hearts of all. It would mean much to me to find the end of an endeavor that allows my heart to wear a smile. It would be a dream come true.

To date, I find the voice of yesteryears still ring loud with fables about love. I find that many people continue to proclaim that love makes the world go around although one man frowned upon hearing such a proclamation and said, "if that be true then this planet is in trouble". There was also another person who wrote a song about giving fifty ways to leave your lover. Arguably, it served well the down side of mankind's happiness enhancing misery as divorce rates explored like dark storm clouds.

It is my hope and prayer that the words you find as you turn page after page somehow help to reestablish and/or simply make more stronger the flames in the heart you kindle. I have attempted to provide all ages with something that will help explain the goodness in a soul you wish to share with another, the kindness you wish to extend appreciation to, the many reasons you are thankful another share your life and indeed feel truly blessed to say the least.

I hope that I have not failed you. I hope you find my work to be a soothing source of pleasure, somewhat of a reference guide for those having computers wishing to design a personal greeting card or creating a message in a bottle, a plaque for a multitude of special occasions and lots of other cool fun things you can do to plant a pastel smile across someone's heart.

While finding pleasure just reading my words, I hope in sharing them with another person, you will be able to transpose shipwrecked relationship into cozy moments sitting in front of a fireplace filled with reconciliation and for those already experiencing smooth sailing, I hope my words somehow strengthen your patience and tolerance and help to immortalize the forever of your peace.

Have fun!... I do wish you well.

Dedication

I dedicate this project to God
Almighty my creator, my strong pillar, my source of inspiration, wisdom, knowledge and understanding.

He has been the source of my strength throughout this program and on His wings only have I soared.

Reader's Reviews

Edward Jordan's poetry comes from a lifetime of diverse experience and a great deal of love. You can hear in his words that he wants to bring love and light to others. He wrote his poetry from a place of such darkness and despair, and that beauty and pain is there too, but there is also so much hope and a poem for every occasion.

- Joelle Kirtley

When Love Came from the Dark": A Journey of Love and Redemption" is a poignant collection of poetry by Edward Jordan. With themes of nostalgia, love, and redemption, these heartfelt poems offer a unique glimpse into the depths of human emotions and the power of poetic expression.

In "Resurrected," the theme of resurrection permeates the lines as the author delves into personal experiences of rising from the symbolic death, reclaiming hope, and embracing a newfound purpose. Edward's ability to evoke raw emotions through these verses is commendable. Each line carries a weight of introspection and takes the reader through the transformation journey.

In "My Only Wish": the exploration of love through the lens of nostalgia. The author seamlessly weaves memories and longing into verses that paint vivid pictures of a past connection and lost love. Through words, they capture the bittersweet nature of nostalgia, touching upon the yearning for what once was and the enduring power of love that transcends physical barriers.

While the circumstances of Edward's incarceration may be evident in some poems, their resilience and ability to find solace and meaning in their art shine through. The lyrics offer a sense of hope and redemption, reminding us of the transformative power of self-expression and the capacity for growth even in the most challenging circumstances.

I highly recommend this book for poetry enthusiasts and anyone seeking a profoundly moving and introspective exploration of life, love, and the power of art to uplift the human spirit.

- Joel Aguilar

Certain poems within this collection left an indelible mark on an individual's soul, evoking such intense emotions that tears flowed unabatedly. Jordan's ability to establish an intimate connection with every reader through their poetic compositions is a testament to the profound impact of their work. Each poem compels introspection on life, prompting contemplation about the need for change and the potential divergence from our personal missions in this world.

In every verse, Jordan encapsulates the indescribable surrender to God—a sentiment that often defies adequate expression but finds solace within these poems. Most strikingly, the palpable adoration for life imbues these verses. The author's profound gratitude to God radiates through each sunrise, rainfall, sorrow, and boundless joy. Simultaneously, he deftly

acknowledges life's fragility, embracing each fleeting moment with unbridled appreciation. This profound sentiment is inescapable within his work.

-Professional Book Critic

You're my World

What would you do if you met an Angel?
What would you do if someone overwhelmed you?
What would you do if you heard a familiar voice
If you turned to speak and you could not…
Tell me what a man is supposed to do.
When he's guilty of loving you.
When friends all whisper he's a fool.
For letting his foolish heart be the one to choose.
It's strange because a cheating man would be excused.
People would understand saying his feelings were true.
Well no matter what the world say about what I do,
I still think there's something special about you.
It's something that moves me day n' night.
It's something that keeps me in a groove.
To my soul you're like rock n' roll music.
Thinking about you makes my spirits dance.
Even in my dreams I find the beauty of romance.
In all four seasons, in you I find the springtime of life.
The freshness of the air I breathe.
In my heart with each thought I search for ways to please.
Because nothing is life without you.
You're my stars, you're my sunshine, you're my sky.
You're my world.

Witchcraft and Magic.... It's Extraordinary

A portrait of a bronze star
That's what you are chiseled to perfection.
A work of art cut from a piece of marble stone.
Naked beauty sculptured by the Gods.
In a crowd you stand alone unabridged with shame.
In plain view sexy lingerie obviously embellishes your frame.
It's definitely certain, a multitude of minds go insane.
In your presence many eyes stand aglow with secret desires.
As bodies collide, whispered apologies permeate the air.
Emotions flare like storm clouds before the rain.
Stirring up an avalanche of mixed reactions.
Even chirring birds get the full of your backfield in motion.
Shakin' and bakin' energizing the hearts of adolescence.
Magically without even a pill revitalizing convalescence.
Just looking sweet usually a weekend occurrence,
But with you it's even in the middle of the week.
Abound with reason traffic, slowly crawls down busy streets.
It's extraordinary witnessing a prance suited in painted on jeans.
I swear, it's got me practicing witchcraft and magic.
Trying to discover ways to plant you on my team.

The Shield of your Love

The comfort no doubt.
You're someone truly special.
You're someone I truly need.
For many reasons, I know your love for me is pure.
In times of sorrow, my heart you let not it bleed.
When I'm down on my knees with prayer,
The spirits I feel, I feel the same for you.
The warm gentle breeze of your love is like magic.
Though at a great distance, nightly I feel it caress me.
I feel its starlight beauty watching over me.
It's like a heavenly beacon lighting my path.
Forever ensuring me safe passage through difficult times.
So I fear not the evil of the dark.
I know the shield of your love protects my heart.

Everything is Gonna be Alright

It's been a bloody battle.
From hell to heaven.
It's been like climbing an insurmountable mountain.
Rocky terrains made the journey more rough.
Trials, moments filled with the smell of death.
Often gave genuine cause to believe,
That of love there was absolutely nothing left.
Not an ember to stir.
Not a crumb from a King's table.
Day was another night.
Dreams of being bathed in river of light,
Were harnessed with nightmare screams.
Screams emanating from pains deep down in the pit of lost souls.
Struggles to start a new life were to no avail.
Efforts were useless in the absence of a much needed power to control,
The evil forces in life we try to avoid.
The power to plant a soul in new soil.
Daily or maybe it was nightly,
Your prayers, your pleads, drifted like smoke riding the wing of hot air.
It was the sum total of your dark.
There exists no compassion– only another broken heart.
The situation was completely clothed with catastrophic fabric.
It was ugly, mean and cold.
Nobody cared! Still there was mystery.
An inexplicable kind of mystery.
A mystery that somehow permeated the air.
The strangest part was that Spirits all seem to have deaf ears.
Forever encouraging the mind to focus.
Willing the soul to believe.
Though in captivity we may be forced to live in the dark.
Crawling in hell like ants on the ground.

The persecution though wrong,
For good reason we must fight to be strong.
As Dr. Martin Luther King Jr. did, I too, had a dream.
A dream that wasn't filled with nightmare screams.
I had a dream I was touched,
That I ascended to a Kingdom that was embellished with bright lights.
Where a voice said, "Welcome, my child.
I am Lord Jesus. Everything is gonna be alright."

In Hell on Earth

When I was a child,
In the midst of my innocence,
Love walked out the door on me.
There were no hugs in my life.
There were no birthday celebrations.
Just another disappointment each year.
My favorite song was "I love you".
I cannot remember a time it romanced my ears.
The sky many find sunshiny and blue,
It was like the geese in the wintertime- to the north they flew.
My soul was left in the hands of evil.
The love of a mother I knew stood in the distance
A grandmother that seemed blinded by my presence,
For much was the patriarch's abuse.
An abuse that touched not just my body but my inner soul.
It penetrated the surface and the heart of my existence.
Like raindrops in a mighty storm penetrating the land.
Scream after scream after scream found no answer.
I don't really know love.
I've looked upon the sky many times.
I've seen what I thought was its twinkle.
I've seen its light brighten the path of a few.
I've dreamed many times that the cold in my soul,
The warmth of its light would one day be found.
Maybe I was just having a fantasy.
Maybe it was just all in my mind.
Still, I've stood on mountain tops.
I've stood in the middle of open pastures
Trying to make myself easy for love to find.
All of my efforts have proved to be useless.
My family, especially my older sibling, I can more easily tell.

She has lived harboring feelings equated to some form of hate.
My son seems to share their feelings, too.
Perhaps, there's some form of hidden justice.
The situation often frightens me.
I sometimes wonder if my destiny is hell.
I wonder if at birth, was I some reason secretly cursed?
Though I question not these dark thoughts for an answer my soul thirst.
For the most part, the Sages of the heavens must know my heart.
Indeed, purgatory awaits my soul with favor.
As wholeheartedly, I trust in those above.
Though I have lost!
I continue to trust I will be found by love.
I pray!
In hell on earth my soul will not stay.

Heart of Gold

It all sounds rather simple.
Lots of people are probably really thinking.
But for me without even blinking,
My love for you will stand and test the flames of hell.
For the many wonderful things you have done for me.
I do pray you never experience what I'm going through.
Unless somehow a miracle smiles down on you.
I wrestle with difficulty almost daily.
Though still I count myself a lucky man.
The things you need from me as a woman,
I welcome the moment to show you how much I understand.
How much I appreciate the many ways you've freed my spirits.
The way you resurrected my hopes.
The way you've given new meaning to my life.
Absence using witchcraft or dope.
The way you use your love relieves my pain.
I'm thankful in many ways for all of you.
You've really allowed me as a man,
To embrace something much greater than financial gain.
It's been a rough road, but you've truly lightened my load.
I feel a comfort throughout my entire soul.
I swear, all because of you.
A girl with a heart of gold.

A Little Wonder

You sometimes think of me.
In your letter that's what you said.
You could be just messin' with my head.
Still you made me smile.
You did much to warm a lonely heart.
You had me doing lots of thinking for a while.
I've been wondering if it's right to let you know,
To you my feelings are something I'd like to show
I think you're the star missing in my sky.
I think you're really quite a courageous fighter.
In my galaxy your future is guaranteed to sparkle brighter.
I see riches in your future diamonds and pearls.
I see myself chasing my dreams, as you are my kind of girl.
It's almost as if I already know you.
Perhaps, you were a Queen, and I am your King in another life.
I wonder, maybe you were my soulmate or maybe my wife.
It probably all sounds somewhat ludicrous.
Though still in a raging sea of hell...A Little Wonder!
Is the boat that keeps me from going under.

Loving You

It's all the time,
The colors of the rainbow so pretty in the sky,
Reminds me of the beauty I find,
Whenever I look into your eyes.
Something magical happens.
When you smile, my heart finds something refreshing.
Dreams all come true when we touch.
The warmth of a pleasant wonder fills my soul.
When we cuddle, when we kiss, when we hug,
No matter the location, I'm at home.
A halo I've yet to witness.
Your wings I've yet to find.
Still of certain I am you are an Angel.
A recipe of pure goodness.
For never before you, has sunshine ever caressed me at midnight.
Your presence is simply a testament,
God has truly touched my life.
So please know that I am forever grateful,
To have been chosen as the one worthy of loving you.
It's simply divine to have you for a Valentine.

In Loving Memory of a Superman...
In the eyes of my Heart a Hero!
To a Child... A Giant!

I used to live in a dream land.
As a child...
The hugs, the kiss were really big treats.
In their absence I felt a teardrop caress my cheek.
For in the moment time so seemingly was an enemy.
Despair somehow negated my real reach for answers.
In the midst of my plight.
Strangely, moonlight became my only sunshine.
Oh lost was I in the dark of its existence.
Remarkably, a whisper endearing in nature,
Magically danced upon the wings of the wind.
Though in awe, it made me strong
Wide open came the doors to my heart.
Suddenly, for the gift of life, my soul swelled with appreciation.
The troubles of which had plagued my yesteryears,
I sought blame for no one. I wanted forgiveness for all.
A big person now though still a child,
I wanted my Giant but he was gone.
So I prayed if there were differences.
I will truly know.
Embodied not were they ever within my heart.
As those eyes that look down upon the flower your seed grew,
Please know the nourishment from your sunshine and rain I still need.
Distance no matter the many miles,
It will never be greater than the spirit of my reach.
For my Giant, though immortalized within the spirit of my soul,
Forever is the time I shall miss you.

I Chose Death

I dreamt I went to hell.
I found myself in an intense interrogation.
The end report invoked an intense litigation.
In the midst of the Devil's court.
The atmosphere smelled of evil; it zapped me completely of my strength.
It left my soul feeling cursed.
I was found guilty.
Being charged with not loving the Prince of Darkness first.
Thereupon, the bargain was clear and simple.
Denounce my love for you,
Or tortuous flames would burst my soul like a pimple.
I was petrified, I did not want to die.
Though when I considered what would be left,
Living a life without you,
It was then I chose death.

Happy Valentine's Day

Daily, I sit staring at a picture.
A beautiful picture.
A picture that hangs on the walls of my heart.
Your silver smile gives me lots of happy thoughts.
You make me feel so close to my dreams,
They have to come true.
I swear, You bring out the best in me.
There's nothing to be a shame about.
With you! There's nothing to lie about.
Sometimes I'm so turned on, when I look at your picture,
I have to move around.
I find myself so excited, I actually start jumpin' up and down.
In lots of ways you astound me.
Especially when you've got your arms around me.
Or when I'm chasing you in a fantasy.
When you hug me,
I know all my prayers are answered.
When you kiss me,
I feel all wishes granted.
Even my darkest moments,
Are filled with blue skies and sunshine.
That's why I know I'm hooked on you.
In the midnight hours, when it comes to loving you,
For some of the things I think about doing,
It might even be a crime,
Still, it's so exciting having you as my Valentine.

Come Listen to my Heart

In hope, captivated will be your interest.
I dreamt, I was traveling through a galaxy.
Speeding along in a rocketship gliding through dark space.
When I looked out the window, there you were.
A star hanging in the sky twinkling like a diamond.
Your sparkle shimmered bright and beautiful.
We were miles apart- though you seemed so close.
I reached out, for I could still feel your light touch me.
I first pondered the possibility of a curse.
Until I heard a soft whisper say you've been blessed.
You've been welcomed to a unique universe.
I felt suddenly foolish, something boyish tickled my soul.
Nervous, I laughed out loud.
I wondered if I had just failed some sort of test.
I welcomed some form of communication.
Silently, I entreated the masters of your constellation.
I pledged myself to servitude if they would but not take you away.
For I wanted to dance with you.
I wanted to marinade in your closeness.
I wanted to laugh with you.
I wanted to brisk in the warmth of your brightness.
I was simply impressed with finding a dream.
I was happy, it felt like your charms had been all scattered
Scattered across the entire land of my soul.
I truly felt like a grasshopper in the middle of springtime.
I felt an attempt to exist without you would be tragic.
I felt it would only be an invitation to death.
Since of my life without you there would be nothing left.
So I pray you listen to my heart.
For I ask to be enclosed in the twinkle of your brightness.
To avoid an existence in the dark.

Society Girl

Like the dawn, even the sunrise,
Your entrance graces the world with beauty, too.
Your poise drips with a fresh infectious charm.
The elegance of your manner smiles with kindness.
The kind that creates an enormous amount of wonder
Your mystery is simply like the rain from dark storm clouds…
You drench the hearts and souls of many.
Rulers and Kings even Philosophers and Queens bear witness,
To your vast field of intellectual properties.
You're so inspirational, so beautiful in so many ways
Touching is the peaceful warmth you wear as you welcome life each day
Your magnetic smile sparks with the innocence of a child
It lifts my spirits up high; it fills me with fairy tale curiosity.
Your laughter reminds me of a whisper romancing a star.
It's truly refreshing the brightness of you.
Never do you ever seem to rush.
Of truth, that part sometimes distresses me.
Because of my thirst, my hunger for our fingertips to touch.
Of our worlds, great is the distance that holds us apart.
Still, in my longing, I hope for you to understand,
My wish for the dream to come true at this very moment.
That finds us writing our names in the sand.
The difference in our worlds perhaps makes greater the risk,
Though still there is nothing I would not do,
To seal our existence with a kiss.

When I Dream

Many are the moments thoughts of you become my dreams.
It seems I can feel myself reaching for you.
To rest my head upon the softness of your breast.
Therein I find a safe haven.
A quiet place so distanced from harm's way.
I find a soothing warmth.
The blanket of your breathing dissipates the chill.
A tempest attempting to torture my body, my everything.
It's like knocking on the door of comfort.
Smiling, you welcome my weary soul unconditionally.
It's no surprise that your generous nature simply continues.
To forever extend an insurmountable measure of hospitality.
Second to none, not even the heavens are a match.
To onlookers your ways are truly a diadem of beauty.
Because of this, my dreams are greater than paradise.
They're like love excursions with butterfly colors.
That's why I dread the moments embraced by the hours of dawn.
Because whenever I dream, we're forever a team.
Like the birds that fly south for the winter...
We fly united.

You're Truly an Angel

Deep down into the roots of your soul,
I don't believe anybody truly knows who you are
I just know that each time you smile,
I witness a twinkle, twinkle of heavenly stars.
I even see rainbows sliding across midnight skies.
You're simply a mystery to the world.
No one knows what you're really made of.
Though, obviously, it's something special from up above
Perhaps, with words it's not so easy to define
But even the blind will attest to your celestial substance.
To your majestic style, your exquisite taste.
You seem to excel in splendor with time.
The Gods of the universe I thank so much.
For I'm so glad you're mine.
A real lady with excellent use of discretion.
Be it a man, woman, or child.
You seem to always ensure an abundance of satisfaction.
The way you so easily procure positive reactions.
Even in a crowd you're like a jewel so sought after.
Never loud, you're the girl that makes a man proud.
You're the girl that adds to the many reasons,
I keep really praying you understand,
Why I'm so happy to be your man.

Just Tell Me

You used to tell me I was the one.
Who held the keys to your heart.
You used to tell me,
You loved the romance and all the kisses,
I used to shower you with when we were in the dark.
You used to tell me,
Our love was the gift God sent,
That faithfully you'd always be there for me.
But now that something has changed my fate.
Now that you've decided to go away,
Can you just tell me,
Why your laughter is no longer my symphony.
Can you just tell me,
What happened to our melody?
The birds chirped from the trees.
Can you just tell me,
What you meant when you said you'd be there for me.
I know sometimes in life there comes a change.
But through it all I swear,
I never thought you'd be the source of my pain.
Maybe I should have seen the writing on the wall.
When the seasons of your love changed from summer to fall.
A foolish man I was. That I will admit.
To believe a Bad Boy's reputation would allow me to find,
The kind of girl that would never quit.
But if this is true price I gotta pay,
Then I just wanna say...
I never meant to hurt you a single day.
So, can you just tell me?

A Beautiful Sunrise

Each morning just before the break of dawn,
You're a busy bee.
Nudging tiny tots with the warmth of a love,
That makes their little eyes shine like tiny light bulbs.
A beauty accentuated by only little quizzical smiles.
Exuding with a love only a mother would know.
It is the love song that romances your heart.
As you reach for utensils to prepare the fuel,
That helps initiate the beginning of their daily journey.
It's remarkable how even the wildlife awake from their slumber,
To be touched by the likes of you.
Priceless is your warmth, the likes of your love.
More valuable than the riches men take from the earth.
Both day n' night you enrich life with goodness.
No one can deny you're a gift from the heavens.
For like twinkling stars, you're forever bright
It swells my heart with elation to know God is so wise.
Because you are of certain a beautiful sunrise.

How I Fell for You

The first time my eyes chanced upon you,
Though distanced, you stood out from the crowd.
Bright like a twinkling star.
In an instant, you shattered my thoughts.
Your beauty simply arrested all of my senses.
It captivated and held me prisoner.
As if you had me locked into a beam of light.
I swear, it felt like something extra-terrestrial.
Though in truth, the situation is ineffable.
In a fleeting second, a million times
I must have questioned myself.
Trying to assign you to a habitat of contemporary times.
Your style of dress gave credence to something medieval.
Though still my heart pounded.
Ignoring any and all signs of possible evils.
For if in fact you held the forbidden fruit,
I was ready to sin.
You were an exact replica of an Angel,
I had heard described by the wisemen.
So in life whatever you decide to do,
Just believe how I fell for you.

I Ask Not

As my soul stands in the shadow of darkness,
No one knows of its battles.
It struggles to find light at the end of a tunnel.
But like a mighty warrior on and on it goes.
Step by step pounding the earth with a relentless determination,
To find and hug the beauty of tomorrow.
In retrospect, I marvel as I gaze upon yesterday.
The love songs of its laughter I still remember so well
Though because of the current storm clouds I wonder.
Sometimes if today is but an egregious scheme of some sort,
Meant to distort my vision and diminished the strength of my faith.
A faith of which flows like raging winter mountains streams.
Of heaven's mercy in prayer, I ask not.
Of the riches men extract from the earth, I ask not.
Of accolades perhaps deserving of terrestrial deeds, I ask not.
I do give great thanks to all for their empathy.
Though I ask not that your heart be permitted to fill with sympathy.
For today I walk free of pain.
As I brisk in a new life, embossed with the Lord's name.

Happy Anniversary

Throughout the many golden years spent loving you,
There have been many happy times.
There have been many tears.
Though we survived the rough parts,
Simply protecting one another with our hearts,
We faced the many challenges in life,
Proudly standing hand n' hand.
Me, your husband.
You, my wife.
Successfully we fought our way through a jungle.
In a world that seldom offered peace.
But in its midst, because the love in our hearts,
Swelled as if it was full of yeast,
We rose to the occasion with each battle.
Forever withstanding the test of time.
Because of you, I stand today thankfully blessed.
To enjoy the beautiful sunset of life.
To embrace that which allows a man to be free
For the spirit of your love truly makes it a pleasure.
To wish you a happy anniversary.

Just Trying to say Thanks

I could write a million words or more.
Though still fall short of an adequate number.
To indicate your score.
For the many wonderful ways.
You've touched my heart.
Your light has shielded me from the dark.
I am truly grateful and indeed blessed,
To be a branch from your tree.
My thanks are many and forever is the time I pray,
To embrace the moment I make you proud of me.
It's because of you!
I am able to eat when my stomach growls.
It's because of you!
I am able to help another as a parent does a child.
I've entreated the Lord for words,
Still I cannot express the measure of my gratitude.
So please! Do try to imagine the size of my thanks.
In return for the many things you do.
Because I really do appreciate you.

A Sunrise

When you smile,
Flowers blossom like it's springtime.
Children's hearts fill with joy.
My soul sits in wonderland.
If I could have you for myself,
I'd make a brand new start.
I'd give you all the love,
The good Lord ever poured into my heart.
I'd make sure you felt exactly what it really means,
To have a true Knight in shining armor on your team.
I'd be your moonlight,
Your sunrise, and everything in between.
I swear!
Your life would be like a good dream.
A fantasy.
Every day I'd give you the best of me.
I'd give you the world.
I'd give comfort to your soul.
The kind that really, really pleases.
I desperately want to be with you.
Often I wonder...
If I could have the last dance.
If I could be the one you spend a lifetime waking up saying good morning to.
Be the man that rubs your back when you say it's sore.
Being in your world,
Would be like a little boy lost in a candy store.
Everyday life would be sweet.
Like now... Loving you from a distance is fun.
Except when the stars twinkle at night,
I need to hold you close.
To whisper in your ear.

To show you how much I care.
Just thinking about it.
How good you make me feel.
The way you make my heart shout.
Makes me feel alive.
Makes happy tears fall from my eyes.
Even in the midst of midnight,
In you! I see a sunrise.

I Speak Honestly

Sometimes I go day after day.
Wondering!
If the one thing I've ever wanted the most,
Love!
Will ever be mine. For years!
I've admired and felt close to you.
I've wished on many stars.
I've hoped for dreams filled with wisdom.
That could guide me toward your trust.
Toward how to change myself into the kind of man,
That You would respect the most.
The kind of man heart would happily endeavor,
To drench with the raindrops of your love.
The kind of man you'd look upon as special.
At least half as special as you've always been to me.
A thousand times…
Maybe more!
I've asked the heavens to touch me with the magic,
That allows one heart to speak to another heart.
The magic that allows you to see clearly,
That by order of the wisemen,
Those that control the skies,
Our destiny, our fate in this world there was meant to be,
A you and me.
Through answers sent from a higher power,
Your fears shall be erased.
So I asked with the fingers of my heart crossed,
That you close your eyes with me in prayer.
Let the spirits of our hands join.
Let your heart whisper with my heart.
Dear Lord!

Though it is loneliness I feel within,
My heart continues to embrace you as a friend.
Hoping to one day have you on my team.
Indeed, as my Queen.
You mean a lot to me.
I understand that words may be difficult to trust.
But this is an extraordinary situation.
So taking a chance you must!
Put your arms around this opportunity.
Erased my anxiety, let my dreams come true.
My fantasy!
Please help stabilize my life.
In all earnestness, I speak not selflessly.
I speak honestly!
I welcome you as my wife.

It's Forever

Whenever I see you,
I believe magic strikes my world.
My spirits brighten like lightning bolts in winter storms.
I hear a blast of rock n' roll music fill my soul.
I struggle to be good, to keep control.
But it's no use, an ocean of desires flood my world.
I try to avert my eyes hoping to avoid,
Your discovery of my mischievous thoughts.
Thoughts that create visions making desperate my desires.
Then you smile, It's a battle I know is clearly lost.
It seems you can see right into the core of my existence.
Often I wonder if I've had enough class.
Flight surge, but I'm weakened by watery resistance.
Though I fear imperfection, I crave your attention.
I find much mystery in what crossed our paths
Still, wholeheartedly I welcome your presence.
The way flowers welcome rain and sunshine.
For you wash clean the sadness of dark times.
Your presence excites spirits.
You fill my heart and soul with clouds of laughter.
You truly ease all my pains and I'm truly thankful for each moment.
It's like being the victor in adolescent games.
A sweet treat, you're better than honey and cream.
I cannot begin to fathom all that it means.
But in truth it charms and dazzles me.
To find infatuation, love, and admiration– all on the same recipe.
In sum, I can honestly say,
Whenever the eyes of my heart visit the sight of you,
It's forever! I wish for you to stay.

On My Street

I watch from within.
As a sunshine glare caresses the window panes of my heart.
I witness how each brush stroke of your foot fall,
Paint the world with your elegance ever so beautiful.
It's remarkable, but in truth it's another wonder.
For I find pastel colors in your smile alone.
So very perfect, no one can justly deny,
Its brightness, the rainbow across the morning sky.
Entrenched, I am by the grace of your stride.
Still my heart journeys the distance of your soft skip.
Such as the wisemen did a star to ensure I never miss,
The glamor you give the dawn.
An early riser I am, with coffee in hand.
I sit awaiting a fairy tale romance with life.
One that makes me jealous of the gentleness of a summer breeze.
The warmth of a flame.
Your mystery no one knows and no one understands it.
Though second, there stands the fragrance of a rose.
As the wind announcing your coming blows its mighty trumpet,
And birds chirp melodies from the trees.
As you prance, you increase the cadence of my heart's beat,
You beautify my day leaving me proud.
As you approach the finish line on my street,
I smile!

With Every Breath

I cannot imagine,
What God was thinking when he created you.
To guess, I would say it had something to do with the stars.
He had the moonlight and sunshine on his mind,
Maybe it had something to do with the rose garden.
The heavens all know that he spent many hours.
Creating a multitude of beautiful flowers.
I don't really know what happened.
I just know never before not even in a dream,
Have I ever witnessed the likes of your smile.
I swear, not even on the face of a child.
When I look at you something incredible happens.
Your eyes shine with a charm that melts my heart.
I wouldn't be surprised,
If the world was a box of Cracker Jacks,
To find you inside as the prize.
For in you I found a heaven on earth.
A magic wand that erased my curse.
You turned my life completely around.
You made dreams come true,
When my hope was in the lost and found.
So with every breath I take,
I'll be loving you.

Imprisoned in Life

Many are the times,
The dawn looks upon fleeting hopes.
Hopes escaping down empty trails chasing empty dreams.
Like raging waters flowing down mountains streams.
Therewith stands a weary empty soul.
Silent as a caged bird listening to its heart quiver.
The storm continues to darken the sky.
Winds blow hard as raindrops fall from lonely eyes.
The moment finds a great distance,
The day is colored forever.
Tomorrow will be the twin child of yesterday.
For lost in the dark is the purpose.
Condemned to doom so seemingly a fate, a destiny.
That obscures a much needed, a much sought after beauty.
Found in the many portraits hanging on the walls of a memory.
Even in a fantasy, solitude becomes an enemy.
It empowers sadness allowing its daggers to plunge deep.
Into the dark existence of each plight rattling life.
Yes, it's an end, perhaps where death is likely the prize.
In earnest, occasionally harnessed with great fear.
Wonder does so seemingly tracks my demise.
My breath sometimes welcomes the dark thirst for human souls.
As time savagely continues to take its toll.
In prayer made are attempts to humble the winds.
Hope entreats the storm.
To extend the life of candlelight still aflamed.
As I witness the next generation bindly forge ahead,
Toward the autumn of its years,
I pray for the day,
Tenderness finds reason to silence my screams.
Reason to transfuse the nightmare with pleasant dreams.

My Peace....
My World!

The years come and go.
But in you, I continue to find a fun life.
The real American dream.
The essence of the pursuit of happiness.
Throughout the years, I've had the privilege to witness,
A hundred or more reasons why I fell in love with you.
Every time my thoughts land on you I again witness,
Why sunshine touches my soul even in the dark.
Whenever I'm plagued with the distance that makes my blood rush.
It's easy to see exactly why I miss you so much.
Though when we are apart,
Thoughts, visions, and dreams of you surge through my heart.
It's ecstasy, an encore of events that romances my memories.
For want of you, my soul screams.
As if I'm a fish flopping around on dry land.
And you're my rivers and streams
My complete sanity! My peace!
The nutrients that keep me healthy and strong.
The reason I'm never weak.
It's because of you, I live a happy camper.
A spirited, gentle man both day n' night.
Giving thanks to our Lord.
For touching me with the rays of his light.
I am grateful!
For blessing me with you.
So I do hope you understand...
My reasons for fighting so hard to be your man.

If My Heart Could Speak

The lights are down real low.
The music is still playing slow.
But for some reason, I have been embraced by loneliness.
What on earth am I supposed to do?
The last dance was supposed to be with you
Though somehow, I've missed my chance.
This must be a bad dream; how could this have happened.
How could my date be associated with sadness...
My goodness if only my heart could speak
It would tell you,
Why the stars and the birds follow you around.
Because just like me they, too, long to be close to you.
To say good morning when the dawn awakes.
To say goodnight after the sunset.
If my heart could speak,
It would thank you over and over again.
For the mere beauty of your heart.
The kindness you always showered on me.
The love, countless times you proved, would never quit.
Oh boy! If only my heart could speak.
It would tell you my soul and spirits are still strong.
You're the reason they have good memories to feed on.
The reason my wishful heart has hope.
Hope that one day you might just come home.
If only my heart could speak...
For our tomorrow, you would know how much I pray...
If only my heart could speak

Happy Birthday

Did I ever tell you,
You're the reason love filled the void in my life?
The reason my spirits soar so happily and out of control.
The reason my life, that once had no direction,
Now has a constructive goal.
To commemorate your birth.
Simply reminds me of the golden moment,
The heavens erased my curse.
In the Cracker Jack box of life,
You were the prize.
You were the sole reason I grew strong.
I grew tall like a tree
Able to stand on my own
Able to weather a mighty storm.
Able to at least make a fatherly effort
To shield you from life's harm.
Your birthday will forever be a golden moment in my heart.
No matter the distance that holds us apart.
Thoughts of you continue to swell me with pride
It's a feeling that truly brings tears to my eyes.
All because I love you.
You're my world.
Even after my demise, you'll still be my little girl.
You're simply special in a special way.
So do understand what it means to me,
To say Happy Birthday.

Of You!... I Need More

When I think about my life,
When I think about the many things that makes me happy,
When I think about the things I would dedicate myself to.
I think about you!
I find myself alive and painted with discovery.
You're my wish...
You're what I pray for.
You're the dream that brings me happiness.
You're my Juliet, Mona Lisa and Cinderella, too.
You're the reason even my fantasy comes true.
You're like something from a wonderland.
You're magical!
Just like the moonlight that brighten a forest at midnight
You're my lucky star.
You light my way in the dark.
The way you touch me with your smile excites my heart.
It excites my soul,
Like toys do kids on christmas.
In your arms, I enjoy the way you take control.
The way your kisses dissipate misery and gives me peace.
I swear, though each moment seems a lifetime with you,
One lifetime is not enough to love you.
Of you! I need more.

I'm Still Standing

Eyes of wonder!
May query the soundness of mind
Still deep rooted are my feet standing in line.
Awaiting the moment like the handsome prince.
The moments that are perfectly right.
To plumber the sweet lips of Snow white.
To taste her kiss.
To feel the warmth of her hug.
To waltz to slow dance with genuine love.
To hear the soft whisper from somebody who cares.
Somebody special that sees me in the picture shows in their heart.
As a twinkling star.
When others see your role as some insufficient part.
I want to feel the warm rays from a special smile.
The one with the beauty of a stellar personality.
The one that blesses the poor as they do the rich
The one inflamed with a natural grace and style.
So I'm still standing.
Faithfully believing in my dreams.
That somewhere on God's green earth.
There's someone special waiting to love just me.
Gently, the way an autumn breeze caresses falling leaves.

Mistakes.... I Make

If you would just give me a sign.
Anything that inflames the smoldering embers of hope,
No wind or rain.
No winter storm could stop me from coming to you.
Nothing could alter my mission.
Nothing could change the way I feel about you.
It would take divine intervention.
For I am yours! Signed, sealed, and delivered.
In body, spirit and mind, I implore you.
To rescue me to cease my heart's quiver.
To ease the fear of facing tomorrow without you
To stop the raging rivers of nightmares,
That twist and splash up against the rocks of my soul.
Let your heart plant me amongst the flowers,
In the garden you tend each morning.
When you smile let me feel the warmth of your sunshine.
When the wind blows let me feel the caress of our soft touch.
Just once more let me dance with you.
In the twilight of the lord's hour let me hear your whisper.
I'm wishing on all the stars in the constellation.
My heart is swinging on my dreams.
I pray for the understanding that makes clear what I mean.
For you're the warmth in my fire.
The happiness in my soul's laughter.
You're like the joy a child finds in a toy.
Mistakes I make! But I believe in you.
And life is certainly lonely without you.

Indeed, I Will Honor You

The first time my eyes chanced upon you.
The first time I saw you smile.
The first time you said hello.
I was baffled.
I was shocked by disbelief.
After a lifetime! Believing there was no such thing as love at first sight.
A lifetime believing!
There was no such thing as dreams coming true.
Your encounter struck me with amazement.
Like after the storm.
The beauty of white clouds found dancing across blue skies.
I found God's truth dancing within your eyes.
It was like finding a Leprechaun's pot of gold at the end of the rainbow.
It was incredulous!
I closed my eyes, shaken by the endowment of a divine blessing, a gift
In the moment,
I thought my imagination had plifered my common sense.
I thought it has taken the best from my heart and soul.
I thought of my senses, I had lost control.
I thought this could not be happening to me.
A bad-boy! A complete stranger!
Blessed with the acquaintance of a real Angel.
No! Not a chance.
Only Casanova, and Romeo had been blessed with such a romance.
When my heart did find its voice...
I struggled with what to say.
I felt I had to make a good choice.
Still so many thoughts rushed to the forefront of my mind,
All wanting to be first.
The fear of messing up almost made me feel I was cursed.
I did not want to give you reason to flee.

For some time...I had not been without words for expression.
I had not before encountered such a beauty.
I felt I could not breathe without it.
My mind had always came up with an answer
Never before had my heart been the one that needed to shout.
To voice its secret.
To speak in earnest about its dreams, its feelings.
Until you!
In retrospect you made me wish.
I had taken advantage of the opportunity to advance my academic skills.
I wanted you in my life.
I prayed it would be God's will.
I prayed your presence meant something favorable.
I prayed the heavens had found in me something admirable.
I did not need anybody to tell me, I needed you.
I was sure, at the altar I would say "I Do."
I'm not exactly cultivated with the conventional mannerism you are accustomed to.
Still there can be no greater truth than when I say...
I will love and respect you.
Like a mighty warrior, I will always honor you.

What Love Can Do

I heard a woman say,
I'd rather be picking up bottles and cans.
Than to live without you as my man.
In the presence of all of heaven,
I swear it as a truth...
I'd rather be homeless in the streets with no food to eat.
It's not a lie!
Before I live without you.
I'd rather die.
I know it may sound somewhat crazy,
But Look at what you've started.
Look at what you've done.
There's no way this can end.
We're much much much more than just friends.
Please understand!
You're the air I breathe.
Yes! I know it sounds insane.
But you're like the blood in my veins.
You give me life.
Her words stopped me in my tracks.
In silence, I looked upon her face for a while.
Spellbound...
In awe like a child.
Confused, trying to surmise.
If the love I saw in her eyes was truly her story.
It was difficult to conceive.
She was an Angel!
It was more difficult to believe...
The situation was attached to something divine.
I reasoned, perhaps some kind of a truth.
To help me understand my feelings for you.

Since from out of the dark...
Her words so seemingly crawled from out of my heart.
The moon shone bright upon the night.
Like a beacon guiding a lost ship.
It was strange, but it was a warm romance.
In the wake of the moment,
I hungered for your touch.
In a special way I needed you.
I needed you to squeeze my hand.
I needed to hear your voice give assurance.
I was your man.
In this life as well as the one to come.
The naked truth flowing from her heart, her soul,
Opened my eyes to many things.
How easy it was to cause another unnecessary pain.
To a benevolent heart regardless of the situation,
How important it was to shower it with appreciation.
As I wandered on down the street in deep thought
Suddenly, I realized!
The lady and I had the same story.
I, too, would rather be picking up bottles and cans,
Then to live not being your man.
The story is simple but it's true.
I'd rather be homeless in the streets with no food to eat,
Facing twenty years to life, then to lose you as my wife.
It may seem somewhat crazy to you, but that's what love can do
Life is really no fun without you.
Hell! Diamonds don't even shine.

In You...
    I Believe

Sometimes I ask myself.
Why do I love you so much?
I sit wondering,
How you're able to access so many,
Of my thoughts.
Why you're the sunshine,
In all of my dreams.
Even in the midst of the Evening hours
Where the breath of a midnight breeze
Makes my soul shiver.
I wonder how!
I feel your warmth.
How the taste of your kiss,
Still touch my lips.
My heart quivers with fear.
Haunted by a dark possibility.
What if I lose you.
Still, your closeness gives me
An inexplicable measure of comfort.
Magically......
You!
Like waters flowing through streams and riverbeds,
Gives life and strength to the whole of me.
For years...
I've braved many depraved challenges.
Befriended the dark.
Religiously...
I've discounted my belief in trust.
The honor and love of another.
The light...

The beauty of rainbows embellishing blue skies.
I've discarded...
Come to regard all as a nemesis.
The dawn of tomorrow brings moonlight.
Mystery...
Somehow within the privacy of concrete walls.
The candlelight of hope.
Continues to flicker.
Though for my sins...The Bow n' Arrow continues to target my soul.
My heart bleeds
Still it is in you!
I believe

Forever With You

Memories!
The yellow brick road to my happiness.
With each journey I find you.
Wearing happy smiles.
The day the moments all come with sunshine.
Never is there a storm.
It's like being forever blessed.
Truly a lucky fellow.
The dawn finds me lying side by side
With a real Cinderella.
You!
The rainbow that colors my blue sky.
The stars that beautify my night.
In every love song my heart sings
You're the rhythm assuring the chill of sadness cannot embrace me.
The reason
In my life all four seasons are summertime
Happy I am
Like the grasshopper without a care
Hard at work
Similar to that of the mighty little ant.
Memories...will always remain in my heart.
They're the candlelight.
That fails not to erase my dark
No matter the time, the place.
Where ever I'm at
They ease the pains of my regrets
Stemming from the loss of you.
Memories are the wings of my heaven.
That helps me mend a broken heart.
No matter what others may do.

Edward Jordan

Because of memories, in love I am
Forever with you.

Forever Yours

I don't know if you know.
How much I love you.
I just know that within my heart
There flows a river of unadulterated love.
An ocean of admiration and respect impossible to disguise.
For you touched me in ways not even wisemen can surmise.
You're the best part of my life.
You're the freshness of the air I breathe at dawn.
The sunrise that brightens my day.
You're the twilight that never fails to blanket the sunset.
To ensure the warmth of my nights.
An inkling, I know not what it all means.
But thoughts of you continue to fulfill my dreams
Prayers are answered when I close my eyes.
I see wishes granted.
I see erased the fears of an untimely demise.
For to love you,
To have been loved by you,
Is to be forever yours.

I Promise

Amazing!
Even in the midst of death, pure dark.
You bring joy to everything.
To everybody...
Kids...
The Elderly...
Even the eyes of the wildlife bean
In your presence ...
Each moment feels like hello, good morning.
Your smile warms sad hearts
The way sun rays warm spring flowers
To make them grow.
Only the heavens can possibly know,
Your magic.
The way you give light to the dark.
A raw diamond... Sparkling like a sky full of midnight stars.
Fortitude...tough as steel
Still your words are forever gentle.
As you display the beauty of virgin pearls
Each time you smile.
My heart voice appreciation, genuine thanks.
Though my soul stands totally baffled.
Engaged in suspense.
By law!
It is forbidden to question the heavens.
Yet, mystery continues to loudly scream.
How can a bad boy be endowed, simply gifted.
With the likes of you.
I shall wholeheartedly embrace my blessings,
For whatever reason I am trusted.

When Love Came from the Dark

To have charge of your care.
I shall squander not a moment of the privilege,
To love you.to shield you from all harm.
Daily, endeavor to enjoy life with you.
Fulfilling our dreams, our fantasies
As we journey hand n' hand toward our silver jubilee.
Indeed, I am thankful to those above.
I promise!
You shall forever have my love.

Within My Reach

Sometimes a deep raging sea,
A large body of water may separate you and me.
Its depths no one can tell.
Though large vessels in port dare to sail.
Only Icebergs brave it, patrol it like mountain rangers.
Mammals and birds alike know of its legendary dangers.
Still my endeavor is to build a bridge straight to your heart
No matter the distance
I vow not even storms or tidal waves will keep us apart.
For in many ways you're dear to me.
Your presence alone simply erases my mystery.
You're a true compassion and countless are the times
You've proven yourself an excellence source of company
The whole of me misses your kisses and hugs.
They warm me at midnight like chimney fires.
They give me courage and strength.
When I was lost I used the compass of your love.
As a candlelight to find my way.
I use it the way I've seen you use it to make me strong.
When you found me weak.
The way you used it to change my life.
From something bitter to something unique.
You're the sweet taste in my heart.
Of certain you're my Georgia peach
In lots of ways I'm truly thankful.
You're still within my reach.

The Journey

It's Springtime! The moment for new birth.
Nature brings cause for celebration.
New life comes alive as her beauty blossoms.
The splendor of its glamor is simply astounding.
It cannot be denied when birds assemble in the trees.
For dawn blinks a pitch and the choir chirps a beautiful symphony.
Like magic it fills the air with enchanting sounds.
Smiling with warmth the sun rises to the occasion.
Graciously giving all a standing ovation.
The beginning is forever fun.
But to immortalize the good times there's much work to be done.
In order for two hearts to perpetuate a beat as one.
Be it in the presence of light or in the midst of a storm.
Pleasing the other should precede self.
To safeguard against inflicting harm.
So practice each day.
Leave not thy castle before you embrace each other.
Each night, close not your eyes before you pray together.
Commit to your vows with honor
Approach your obligations with joy.
Welcome your responsibilities with love,
Keep healthy thy spirits
For how you handle trials and tribulations,
Is the clay that will be used to shape your world.
Your adolescent years will eventually become distanced memories.
Therefore with each stroke of life's brush,
Remember to paint the picture beautiful.
Use the pastel colorful warmth of summertime.
Be not ever spiteful, be trustful of each other.
Fight to let the beauty of the autumn leaves be a part of your heart.
For it will lead you surely to a silver jubilee.

Where you will have riches.
Greater than what man takes from the earth.
For you will have been blessed with the gift God gives through birth.
The journey is yours!... Bless you!
Have fun!

Man... I Am

When the sun shines,
When butterflies flap their wings to perfume the air,
When birds sing to your heart,
And romance you with melody to ease your despair,
When your spirits soar with the wind,
And laughter from deep down within rings like wedding bells in June,
When astrological signs say you'll find somebody soon,
Somebody you can really count on,
Somebody that's presence even when you're alone,
Somebody that gives you the kind of love,
When you're feeling weak it makes you strong,
That's when you'll understand the kind of man I am.
The kind of love I'll give when you're in my arms.
For like a kid at a carnival is the kind of joy you'll feel.
I'm the kind of man that believes in the commitment of a vow.
I'm the kind of man that welcomes responsibility.
Like the wilderness welcomes animals that run wild.
So watch out when I'm hungry and you feed me a kiss.
Because I swear the things I do,
Will really prove how much I appreciate you.
I'm a one woman's man.
I believe strongly in the Lord.
And though many may not share my views,
Believe me even if the world stopped,
there 'd still be me and you.
That's the kind of Man I am.

Those He Bless

Many are the nights,
Sleepless, I lie wrestling with distress.
My heart drowns in the dark waters of regret.
It's you! My life raft I truly miss.
I remember the warmth of your smile.
I remember your laughter alone transfused my sadness.
I swear never before have I ever known such happiness.
I thought it was witchcraft and magic.
The way the sparkle in your eyes erased my loneliness
The way my spirits blossomed with exuberance.
The excitement I felt from your closeness.
Yes, you were the miracle, the prize.
I cannot believe my foolishness caused me to take the risk.
Though perhaps damned for life.
There still lies a joy in my memories as I reminisce.
So forever shall be the time I pray.

Just Wanna Make You Mine

My heart has been saying for a long long time,
Don"t let me catch you in the rain walking.
Don't let me catch you far from home alone.
I've been waiting for a chance to be gettin 'at cha.
You've been the main attraction in all my dreams.
It's so strange, now that I've got you in my reach.
You've got me all worked up feeling wonderfully crazy.
Wishing... I was the raindrops falling from a distant place.
Planting kisses all over your lovely face.
A lifetime it seems I've waited,
Still, You've got me spinning around and I just can't stop.
I don't wanna feed you some silly line,
Something that ain't true to make you mine.
Though I will if I have too.
It's not something I practice.
It's just something special about what I'm after.
The situation is serious...
The something that I'm after, It's you!
That's why I'm glad I caught you in the rain walking.
I'm glad I caught you far from home alone
Some way I just gotta make you mine.
I gotta make you my lady.
I know you've got aspirations and dreams, too.
I'm not trying to make you change.
I'm just trying to say I do at the altar with you.
Cause I'm the kind of man,
That'll kiss teardrops from your eyes.
When it rains, cuddle with you in front of chimney fires.
The kind of man that'll hug you up.
Make you warm and strong.
Especially in a moment when you might feel lost and alone.

I'll picnic with you in the park
Wrestle with you in the grass and never never break your heart.
Yes! I'm the kind of man that likes to please.
And you're the kind of woman I really really need.
That's why I'm glad I caught you far from home alone.
I just wanna have a chance to make you mine.
So C'mon let me kiss you.
PLEASE!

Change Your Mind

If I told you about the pain,
That keeps me awake at night,
The reasons I lie in the dark hugging my pillow tight.
The reason I live in the shadow of the sunrise with a broken heart,
Do you think you could be the candlelight,
To wave the magic wand,
Perhaps give my life a fresh start.
Do you think you could put your arms around me,
Use your body heat to warm my soul.
Where for so long it's been really really cold.
Do you think we could come together.?
Kiss! Maybe we can become each other's pleasure.
Our yesteryears do have smiling moments,
Good memories.
Even though I acted like a fool and really messed up.
I'm sorry...
Please is what my heart screams.
I'm begging for another chance.
I can't sleep
My body feels really weak.
I can't eat.
I hunger for your touch.
In more than a thousand ways I need you.
Your kiss, I need to strengthen my soul.
Your love to erase my dark days.
If by chance you feel you can't love me,
Maybe because of what you feel within,
Somehow won't allow us to be more than just friends
I'll understand, at least I'll try hard to.
I can't lie...
Say I'll be able to stop loving you.

Whatever tomorrow brings I'll still be cheering for you.
You'll always be my Cinderella.
My Juliet, too.
I shall forever hold your glass slipper until I find you.
My heart shall forever stand at the foot of your castle.
Serenading you! Should you change your mind?

Just Take a Chance

I wish I could kiss you.
Hold you real close.
Whisper my feelings to your heart.
Do the things with you many lovers do in the dark.
Erased would be all of my pains.
Just as the sunrise transforms a snowcapped mountain,
Into a perfect picture of nature's beauty,
My life would be forever changed.
Beauty! glamor!
The splendor of a summer garden would color my world.
My spirits would indeed be out of control.
Still, at complete peace would be my entire soul.
On numerous occasions,
I've envisioned us on a honeymoon vacation
In the South of France.
Where the world is said to never sleep.
Like in a wonderland where love permeates the air.
Where nobody has a single care.
There are lots of things to do with you.
Perhaps our union would somewhat explain,
Why am I so deeply enchanted by you.?
Thoughts of you are like the blood in my veins
They give me life.
Pleasure, sound reasons to live.
I pray, asking the heavens to touch your heart.
Let us become one.
Let your care, your safety be my responsibility.
In sickness or good times.
I solemnly promise never to forsake you.
Just take a chance.
Please! C'mon say yes.

Twinkling Star

I wish I could kiss you.
Just one time.
Whisper sweet words to your heart.
Somehow make you mine.
I wish we could fly away on a magic carpet ride.
Somewhere into deep outer space.
With me planting kisses all over your lovely face.
At dawn...
We could bathe in the warmth of the sunrise.
Indeed, love would keep us alive.
Everyday!
We could play upon the Milky way in the cool of the night.
We could dance across the galaxy under the beauty of the starlight.
I swear on everything sacred above.
It would be my endeavor to shower you with all of my love.
So C'mon take a chance on me.
Let me be the one that makes your dreams come true.
Fulfill your fantasies.
In life, I know there's no guarantee, but even thorough dark stormy weather,
You'll be safe with me, and happy, too.
Just let your life be my responsibility.
Some people say a man has a weakness,
When it comes to a woman, but with me it's not a weakness.
I'm just not ashamed to love you.
To tell you how you touch me deep down in my soul.
How it sometimes feels like I lose control.
Plus, you must understand,
There's something magical about you.
The way you love makes me feel like a Superman.
Special, I tell you no lie.
Sometimes, I even believe I can fly.

When Love Came from the Dark

I wanna be a part of you at the end of the day.
I wanna be the man you come running home to.
After all, it's written in the constellation.
You're the twinkling star.
That can make all of my dreams come true.

It's Hell

Often, I find you in my dreams.
Late nights, in the midst of a deep dark,
You're the moonlight I feel crawling on my soul.
Smiling! Pulling me into your arms.
Holding me captive with the warmth of innocent charms.
Your ways...
Your style...
Speeds up my heartbeat.
Like a lost child, I feel it rapidly beating wild.
Still, you fill me with a much needed assurance.
You make me feel as if I've been swallowed up by wonder.
A paradise...
It's like drifting into deep space.
A galaxy...
Your mystery enchants my senses.
Inside your world every day feels like a snow white Christmas.
Your touch infames my spirits.
Like a match creates raging forest fires.
You make me feel alive.
Though parts of me ultimately shakes.
As if naked in the pasture of a winter storm.
For with each tic toc of the clock,
The Dawn, the enemy of my peace approaches.
It's like being just a half of mile from heaven,
Then I'm dropped back into the dark of a cruel cruel world.
It's Hell!
Living life without your smile,
It's living life in a jail cell.

My Heart Screams

I knew the day would come.
I knew angry winds would one day chill my soul.
I knew I would have to pay for what I've done.
In great fear...
So seemingly I've lived for years.
I've pictured the moment,
A sadness would eclipse my joy.
The moment you would discard me.
As if I were a broken toy.
Those seeing big tears falling from sad eyes,
Tears like raindrop in a mad storm,
They would probably empathize.
Or in the least voice a sympathy.
Though in reality...
Never in a million years would they understand.
Even at a King's command.
How undeserving of a tender thought I am.
Egregiously, I romance something sacred.
Something a rational mind would have treasured.
Something revered...
That would have added to the moment of a man's pleasure.
You!
You were the starlight that sat my galaxy aglow.
In my world you were the moonlight.
The beacon that guided life through dark passages.
You were simply beautiful...
The essence of a happiness sought after by something massive.
A plethora of suitors awaited the chance to ask for your hand.
You were a gift from the heavens.
A gift I foolishly took for granted.
I gambled with your affection.

When you needed support I played a wick part.
Senselessly, I broke your heart.
Now I sit lost and alone.
I sit languishing in an empty home.
I sit weak in all the ways I once stood proud and strong.
I wish I could be cherished and loved again.
I wish I could be back in arms that care.
Because each time I close my eyes,
I'm assailed by Demons in another nightmare.
Viciously plunging molten knives into my soul.
Until of all my senses I lose control.
I wish somebody could shake me.
Tell me It's just another bad dream.
Anything that would dissipate the pains.
When My Heart Screams.

A Wishful Heart

I've always wondered what I would do.
How my life would change what it would be like.
To encounter someone as special as you.
I've wondered if I would be able to entice you.
In my solitude I've pictured the moment.
I've witnessed the magnetism of our animalistic attraction.
Though I admire its dynamics.
The way it achieves such positive reactions.
My rap made others sound like a joke.
I fought hard for your attention.
Whatever it took to get the best advantage.
I wanted to make your heart skip a beat.
I wanted to have something to do with the reasons.
You always smiled so sweetly.
I just wanted you to feel being with me was better.
Then a bag of Halloween treats.
I dreamt of kissing little raindrops from your eyes.
I hoped though being a bad boy,
I could somehow still make your heart weep with tears of joy.
I wanted to be a gift to you.
I wanted to be something that made you feel...
Like Christmas and Valentine Day were a part of your birthday.
I would love to give thanks to the heavens in person.
To show the measure of my gratitude and appreciation.
For being allowed to cultivate the soil of your soul.
For being allowed to fertilize your land with the seeds of my ecstasy.
In all earnestness with you when it comes to love,
I want a reputation for being a romantic killa.
I wanna be to you what Micheal Jackson was to Thrilla.
Those are the joys of a wishful heart.

Edward Jordan

A box office winner my movie would be
If only you would play the leading part.

A Life Long Mission

Life would be so less complicated.
So less frightening, so much less lonely,
If only we would share it with one another.
you 'd be the crown to my soul.
I'd be your Knight, someone proud and bold.
It would be more rewarding facing its hardships together.
We could make lots of songs.
Awarding winning melodies number one hits.
One harmony would make life forever and ever more fun.
Just think of a life full of laughter and screams of joy.
It would be an indescrabable paradise, a wonderland.
It would certainly be something special.
Allowing the little drummers of two hearts to best as one.
In our journey we would simply forge ahead hand n' hand.
Thankfully, knowing that we were secured in what we had with each other.
Was a love that could truly withstand stormy weather.
Only the heavens would ever understand.
How thoughts of you became the masters of my plan.
For absence your presence nothing could ever erase my stead.
As a lonely man.
I trust wholeheartedly in the goodness of your ways.
I trust the magic of touch.
I believe not!
The evil of distance could ever make you stray.
Perhaps I did fail to make a decent start.
Still today your name remains tattooed across my heart.
For better or worse I pledge my allegiance to you.
As my soul's intentions,
Are geared toward making our union a lifelong mission.

Dance Wit' Cha

I try to understand.
The love I see in you.
There's something special about it.
I can see that it's true.
I sit sipping a drink watching you.
You got me moving and I can't stop.
When you're teasing and shaking up what you got.
So let me dance Wit' cha.
Let me hold you real right
Let me dance Wit' cha and dance all night.
Cause girl you're so fine.
I can't help what I feel, I just wanna make you mine.
I wanna hold you close to my heart.
I wanna be the reason that you smile when we are apart.
You got me acting like a child with a brand new toy.
But sitting here watching you gives me so much joy.
There's something special about you babe.
I swear it's just turning me on.
So let me dance Wit' cha babe.
Just let me hold you tight.

I'll Never Love Again

Once I gave a love that was really true.
A foolish man.
Instead of putting the good Lord first,
It was you.
You made me believe,
There was something to build a future on.
But the way you put me down in front of your friends,
I should have known love was gone.
Still though it's okay you burned me once
It won't be twice.
I'll never love again.
I'll never have a heart to defend.
Cause only hurt and pain comes in the end.
I've learned the lesson well.
I understand friends don't come before benjamins.
So I'm gonna take each step real slow.
Learn something about girls before I say hello.
If her spirits don't dance way up on heaven's floor.
I'll assume I have enough information to say no, no, no,.
Maybe I might just live my life alone.
Since a taste of happiness, a semblance of joy,
Seems to only find me when I'm on my own.
Though either way it's okay, I've made up my mind.
I'll never have a heart to defend
Cause friends don't come before benjamins
And only hurt and pain comes in the end.
So I won't love anybody else.
I'm just gonna somehow learn to love myself.

I'm Dedicated

I'm the kind of man needing lots of attention.
I suffer from lack of satisfaction.
Yesteryears simply fell short of hugs.
So periodically I have a lustful fantasy.
When I smile I try to present a beautiful attraction.
In return I hope for a positive reaction.
Secretly, I hope you find me hard to resist.
I hope to your soul,
I'm a perfect portrait of something animalistic.
I hope when you look you find ecstasy.
I hope your heart fills with desire to undress me.
I hope you welcome me in your arms.
In fact, find me worthy of favor.
My character, decent and principled I am.
Though still I possess not the charm of Casanova.
I'm more of an ordinary guy trying to holla at you.
As a woman my position I'm sure you understand.
A lonely man who asked not for pity.
I simply ask that you grant me one of many wishes.
That you make someone special a dream come true,
Perhaps together out by an ocean.
Somewhere quiet, building castles made of sand.
Somewhere just watching how you charm the birds.
How you so easily have them eating out of your hands.
I pray for us to grow as one.
For like heat to a flame or a fish is to water.
I'm dedicated.
My wish is simply to be a part of you.
And if you should die and go to hell.
I'd really try to follow you.

Until We Meet Again

A fleeting glance, a brief moment.
Still I saw all of you.
You smiled, your heart whispered a secret.
I heard it's every word.
Your legs, your hips, your eyes all said hello.
As you waved your goodbye.
Your departure left me completely bewildered.
Though full of warmth bursting with admiration.
My heart and soul haggled over your reason.
I wondered why I did not charm you; how did I fail.
How did I not pursue you?
Bewitched by your beauty I do confess.
For the likes of you simply had me transfixed.
I now exist overshadowed by a dark cloud.
I wonder if it is perhaps just doom.
Though still patiently I await the day.
My eyes chance another glance upon you.
For I am now equipped with a plan to seize the moment.
A plan that will make my dreams come true.
So farewell my love until we meet again.

My Balance

In each moment of life there lies balance.
Like with the sunrise.
That warms the chill of dawn.
The sunset that assuages fatigue souls.
And embellish the evening with splendor.
In you I find the beauty of inspiration.
A whirlwind of goodness that drives me.
Be it at a fast pace or a slow one.
you 're the weight in my heart that holds me steady.
The way the earth spins so perfectly in its axles.
You are my balance.
For in peace with an open heart we love.
In harmony with equal portions of self we share.
In retrospect, I remember well.
I was once lost, I was once cursed.
I was a wounded Warrior.
Tumbling like falling stars into empty space.
Until you brushed my soul with a kiss.
And enfolded me in your embrace.
Forever I will appreciate you.
For all I shall forever remain thankful.
For the many ways you used your talents.
Continues to keep me balanced.

Believe In Us....
I Do!

Many have been the times,
When sleep denied me a hug.
When nightmares caused my soul to scream.
When the pains of the presence caused my heart to cry.
Times when I've simply felt lost.
In each moment of despair,
My thoughts somehow crawled.
They reached for you and I found a mountain of strength.
I found a nourishing warmth
A love I could count on.
At first I wondered if it was temporary.
But to date...
The distance we've traveled together speaks the truth.
I'm grateful...
I'm thankful God gifted me with you.
You really are a wonderful one.
Still my journey continues to be plagued with struggle.
You give me more kindness in little ways,
Then I've ever known in all of my days.
In large part because of such...
In the presence of all I hold sacred,
All that I believe in...
I've pledged my allegiance to loving you.
Throughout our good times and hardships.
I shall forever honor God's gift.
You are indeed the better part of my once wearied soul.
So my precious lady...
In the midst of dark moments,
When you're feeling somewhat blue, maybe troubled.
When nothing seems right,

Remember to close your eyes and think about me.
Let your heart call out.
Distance my hold us apart,
But I swear I'm forever here for you.
The spirits of my soul will answer.
They will embrace you…
Just keep your head up…smile.
Life sometimes seems like a long hard road.
Often filled with lots of stumbling blocks,
But rest assured nothing will change our tomorrow
You are my woman.
You're proven like my favorite tree.
During the picnic moments of my life,
You provided me with lots of shade.
During my many troubled times,
Being concerned you've stood through winter storms.
Of certain I am…
You're simply remarkable in lots of ways…
Even if God were to strike me blind, your beauty I would still see.
So I hope, I pray with the whole of me.
That you find ways to understand and trust me.
Believe in Us…I Do!

Still the Same

Didn't get to push you in a swing.
Learn from you your favorite things.
Wasn't there to share your pains.
Yet my love for you is the same.
Couldn't hold your hand and guide you.
Nor from your fears successfully hide you.
You nor I are to be blamed.
My love for you is the same.
Didn't see you when you lost or won.
But was there when and before your journey began.
Encourage you to enjoy both the sun and rain.
My love for you is the same.
Whether or not you feel it.
No other can ever steal it.
You're the greater part of a divine plan...
The first man!
You'll understand included is your given name
My love for you is the same
Your first acts...
Steps, voice, words and smile.
Reside in my mind for a forever.
The struggle to prepare to get you settled on this earth,
Was simply rewarded with your birth.
Though now your ears deafen to my voice.
At least once again you'll have a choice.
To learn how the path began.
Was laid so plain.
My love for you is the same.
It's a love imbued with pleasure and pain
Still it's a love that never changed.

When Evil Rose

It was totally absence of notice
There was no caveat to warn the moment.
There was simply an earth shaking eruption.
A mighty blast came from beneath its crust.
It was like something super volcanic...
As it pasted exterminated walsall in its midst,
Its flames shot up into the sky like a rocketship.
Through dark clouds on a warm summer night.
It traveled soundlessly with the speed of light.
The Knights of heaven were in total shock.
They were amazed by the force of its unexpected attack.
Though they knew the Prince of Darkness was back.
Still as their nemesis came under the cover of dark.
Defensively they found their position somewhat nugatorious
Those of whom had devised the plan for the mission,
Carefully calculated their maneuvers with acute precision
They left nothing to chance.
Their technology seemed like something from an advanced millennium.
Their weapons were equipped with laser guided armor.
Its accuracy was like a King Cobra, a real charmer.
So advanced it turned shock into marvel.
Their weapons could be calibrated within tiny seconds.
The impact of what they generated was simply something tragic.
It was something equated to witchcraft and magic.
No one knew how or why; It was just truly surreal and totally unrealistic.
Its design characteristically was of something futuristic.
The sudden attack left the universe quiet with wonder.
So quiet it seemed all had bowed their heads in prayer.
For a simple knock on a door sounded like a boom of thunder.
Many people abandoned their faith.
They even attempted to ransom their souls for another day.

In answer to their pleas, there was only a loud roaring laughter.
No one had anticipated purgatory before death.
Though as hope flapped its wings,
Clearly heard were the wishes of many hearts as they screamed.
Screamed for the arms of salvation.
In the midst of being overshadowed by a dark revelation.
It was simply a disaster as the story is told.
When Evil Rose.

My Heaven

I cannot say enough about you.
In short, you're my life, breath and everything.
I have no shame for through you peace came.
I survived hell.
Even when stronger men didn't do so well.
Late nights tears often soothe the pain of a few.
But my fears are reposed by many thoughts of you.
They're lyrics that turn nightmares into pleasant dreams.
They relax my soul with a freshness like mountain water streams.
It makes loving you simply more a pleasure.
I swear, the depths and heights of my feelings for you,
They cannot be measured.
For your encounter was a wish that was granted.
You were my dream that came true.
The years have been many since you took me into your care.
I cannot explain the magic of you.
I just know you're greater than my prayer.
You're my heaven, perhaps a mystery.
Though an Angel I know watches over me.

My Tomorrow

When the dawn finds you in my arms,
Loved, showered with kisses, and shielded from harm.
When it finds your heart empty of sorrow,
Then I will have found my tomorrow.
For you're the half that makes me whole.
You're my beginning and my end.
You're the road that leads me home again.
You're also like the star the wise men followed.
You're my beacon!
Your brightness is the compass that gives me directions.
I marvel each time my eyes chance upon you.
You remind me of a beautiful flower.
Your presence is like the rain from dark storm clouds.
You soak the land of my soul with pure happiness.
I would love to be your morning dew, the butterfly or,
The Bumble-bee that pollinates your world.
I would love to be anything that unites me with you.
The lights of your heart if only of it I could maybe borrow,
a second, a minute, maybe an hour,
Then it will definitely be my tomorrow.

A Silly Girl

When we were just kids.
You were really naive but ever so sweet.
I was shy and confused, still you were my treat.
Although it was hard to exert my will.
Whenever I needed to say the things you made me feel
It was each time you smiled.
My heart would shout trying to express the joy found in a thrill.
But simply said the words would not come out.
It was really strange how a silly girl,
So easily had my heart experiencing such intimate chills.
Each time your laughter filled the air.
I wondered about the things that made people stare.
In lots of ways you were simply special.
You made my heart, my soul and spirits dance.
So don't be afraid to be a silly girl.
In large it was your laughter and your smile,
That really attracted me to your world.
Don't be afraid to play in your private world.
I'll accept you as you are.
You don't have to be a celebrity to be my star.
You've been the greater part of the reason for my happiness.
Now that you're a grown up girl,
Friends all say that you're running wild.
They say you're fascinated by gold, diamonds and pearls.
They say you're the talk of the town.
From hanging out with boys driving expensive cars.
They all say you'll never last.
A girl with a reputation for being fast.
I wonder about all the news.
I wonder because when you smile at me
You still twinkle, twinkle like midnight stars.

When Love Came from the Dark

Your personality still has a heart touch flare
Each time the melody of your laughter fills the air.
You still make people wanna know you as they stare.
So don't be afraid to be a silly girl.
You're still the bright lights in my world.

Never Wanted You to Go

I never wanted the spotlight.
I never wanted diamonds and pearls
I never wanted all those worldly things.
You made me happy with just a smile.
The way you touched me with your eyes.
When you wrapped your arms around me.
It drove me completely wild.
You made me love you with just simple things.
Like the time you bought me an engagement ring.
At the store from a bubblegum machine.
Your kisses and hugs gave me joy.
I thought you would understand,
Being the boy you watched grow to be a man.
I really thought you knew it was only you.,
That was the ruler of my heart.
I remember you used to tell me,
I was the flower you loved to smell.
I remember you used to tell me,
If I died, with me you'd go to hell.
I knew you lied.
Though still it was sweet, and I tried to tell you then.
You were the air I breathed.
I tried to tell you,
You were the sunshine that made me grow.
You may find it difficult to forgive me.
It may never even happen.
Still in my heart you'll forever be the star of my show.
So I tell you not these things to say,
Wise counsel did not warn jealousy would drive you away.
I know I did a silly thing.
When I saw that girl smile and flirt with me.

When Love Came from the Dark

I didn't mean to hurt you.
I never wanted you to go.

Missing You

Held hostage is my sunshine.
Storm clouds demand ransom impossible to meet.
Though if I could just hear your whisper.
If I could just be touched by your smile.
If I could just kiss your lips, hold you for a while.
If I could caress your body, rub your feet,
Maybe taste the fruits of your garden so juicy n' sweet,
The emptiness in my heart would fill.
I swear my life would be complete.
For any part of you would be a special treat.
Anything that brings you close to me.
Though still from a distance you somehow ensure my peace.
But in the moment I need to feel your breath upon me.
I need to see my dream come true.
I need my prayer answered for though with each dawn I find sweet morning dew,
Still again I find myself missing you.

I Thank You

Have I told you lately I love you.
Have I told you lately that I care?
Have I told you that within my heart there lies a need.
It's a need requiring me to be close to you.
It's a need, of which constantly craves your presence
Because of this each night I'm down on my knees.
I entreat the Lord hoping to keep you in my life.
For in your absence life is like concrete and steel.
It's hard to navigate in rough waters in an evil world.
So I thank you for the diligence of your concern.
I thank you for your patience, your perseverance.
The goodness of your heart certainly keeps me afloat.
It has served me well as the engine in my little boat.
I also thank you for the love that fortified my hopes.
In all earnestness, I thank you for lots of things.
So in the moment just this once, I hope I'm able to touch your heart.
For the many times you've touched mine.
I thank you!

I Vow

The moment my gaze fell upon the soul of your country,
I found a glimmer of beauty in everything.
I found the contour of your land meticulously sculptured.
You were so perfectly developed I tested your waters.
Though deep they were pleasant and warm.
I rested my weary head upon your mountain peaks.
To my thankful heart your soil was soft n' sweet.
I searched exploring your valley, I found a stream.
Being thirsty I kneeled to drink.
Fresh and cool it was something tropical in taste.
Still to my surprise, there was a semblance to the fruit in paradise.
It was then I vowed.
I will crown you ruler of my heart.
The master of my soul.
The captain to navigate the vessel of my mind.
You shall be the guardian of my spirits.
If you will, but concede to the planting of my seeds in your garden.
I shall solemnly pledge at the fall of autumn's leaves,
I will assist with the harvest.
I will further pledge my allegiance to ensuring your comfort.
Question not, shall you ever find my integrity.
Second to none shall you ever find my servitude.
At the dawn of twilight I shall enter your chamber,
To attend my duty massage your soul, and your feet.
Before each sunrise I shall plunder the honeycombs.
To ensure your coffee or tea is sweet.
I will strive to fill your life with splendor.
I shall forever bestow upon you,
Only that of which true love can render.
I vow!

The Breath of Me

Often your passion makes my temperature rise.
It warms me inside.
It feels like morning sunshine.
Then when your smile touches my heart,
Often I feel lots of little raindrops fill my eyes.
In many ways you're simply beautiful.
Special is an insignificant description of you.
It should only describe the way you say hello.
I wonder sometimes if I'm dreaming, if I'm still alive.
Did the heavens really make you mime.
My situation feels remarkable.
When I close my eyes I can actually feel myself.
Soaring like a bird exploring the wonders of our galaxy.
The octane from your sweetness.
Your kindness fuels the Rocketship of my spirits.
The measure of our gentleness rejuvenates my weary soul.
In my heart I cannot imagine another taking your place.
You're simply the breath of me.
The absence of you would bring no surprise.
For I am sure.
It would only be the call to my demise.

The Best Part

You're something special like a bridesmaid.
A diamond amongst precious stones.
No matter where you stand in this world.
Be it in the midst of young girls you're the princess.
You're zestful, the bright light of the party.
Your spirit simply dissipates the dark in other's hearts.
Like magic is the glamor of our smile.
So effortlessly you ease the pains of even a starving child.
The elderly no longer bold though still they are brisk.
It's because of the heated flame of your concern.
On winter nights the year rund.
You somehow touch others like the warmth of chimney fires.
Your gentleness caresses the chills of weary souls.
So daily I search for a lucky charm.
A four leaf clover the magic wand of life.
Anything to stand me in the lights of your favor.
As many are the times I've dreamt you.
I've labored planting my plans around you.
For I would be greatly honored to be your Knight.
The man responsible for protecting you
In my solitude much are the times,
I pray my words will be the song that enchants your heart.
Under candlelight at midnight.
I entreat the Lord for much when it comes to you.
It's like ifever my life found a fresh start,
You would certainly be the best part.

A Winter Season

How do I explain to the other part of me?
Why loneliness continues to be my only company.
Especially, when the absence of your presence,
Continues to suffocate me with misery.
It's quite clear the sights of your perspective
Finds my soul meritorious of punishment.
Though troubled I am trying to fathom its reason.
In all earnestness I know not my crime.
Thus, I implore you to entertain some measure of reconsideration
I ask that the eyes of your favor find my appeal...
Even in the midst of guilt the essence of my supplication,
Due to good cause entrears your heart to forgive.
I ask that you pardon my transgressions with a second chance.
I ask that you once again be my sunshine, my rain.
The recipe and nutrients that makes blossom,
The flowers in the rose garden of my heart
For you're my soul, there is no life without you.
There is no tomorrow.
I pray the heavens guide your decision.
In due time I know the lord will heal your pains.
At the moment my prayers continue also for other reasons.
Not just because my summer, spring and fall all feel like a winter
It's much because I love you.
It's more because I need you as a friend.
It's because I wanna be your man.

It's Time for Me...
             To Face My Fears

In spite of what people were saying,
I couldn't hear.
I didn't listen.
I should have seen it coming.
Even with my heart in pain.
I should have seen it when you changed.
I should have noticed the times,
You looked at me, eyes dripping with shame.
The many times you came home,
Forgot to give me a hug.
The way you turned away,
Never asking if I had a good day.
Foolishly, I told myself.
You were probably just tired.
In all the things I believed in from up above.
I knew for me.
Your heart was full of love.
I convinced myself that of your love,
I was still the winner.
Though each evening after a hot shower,
You would just pick over your dinner,
I would watch you make a short phone call.
I didn't wanna believe it,
But the writing was on the wall.
It was another stab in a heart that was already sore.
Screaming out!
As I watched you silently walk out the door.
Gifting me with another sleepless night.
Another night along with my pillow.
Another dawn to face along with my coffee.

When Love Came from the Dark

Another moment lost in dark contemplation.
Soul shaking with lost hope.
Like leaves on an Oak tree in a winter storm.
Any kind of reason that makes some sense.
A panacea of some kind.
Anything that would assuage my pains.
I gotta hand it to you.,
You had me going for a while.
Hook, line and sinker.
I couldn't even get past your smile.
Praise the Lord!
I got a wake up call.
A heavenly message loudly intimating,
You don't care about me at all,
Love would have brought you home last night.
You would have been with me
I wouldn't be in tears.
Yes! For many good times,
I do think you.
For the many good years.
But Adios Amigo!
It's time for me to face my fears.

I Dream of a Tomorrow

In another time.
In another place.
A heavy hand banged a gavel upon an antique desk.
A desk seemingly from the 16th century made of walnut wood.
My soul grew weak as I stood,
Face to face with my fate.
There from that ancient old desk a deep voice bellowed life.
Suddenly, I lost the use of my heart. It felt like my soul died.
But many years have come to pass.
I'm still alive...
Like a rose bush braving the cold of a winter season.
I dream of a new tomorrow.
When dawn awakes another sunrise.
Above the white clouds that waltz with rainbows across the blue skies.
Like an eagle, I will spread my wings and soar.
Behind I shall leave the shackles and cages.
That for years has imprisoned me.
The authorities that enslaved me. The evil that scared me.
Forward I shall charge into the future.
I shall charge with the wisdom of the Sages
A wisdom that has empowered me.
I shall journey to a new land.
A land filled with adventure, a freedom to love.
A land where the air is permeated with children's laughter.
I shall endeavor to teach the young.
No child shall be left behind. No woman, no elder shall ever be treated unkind.
So it shall be written.
There shall be no hate, no prejudice, no pain, no hunger.
In another time,
In another place,

When Love Came from the Dark

Three shall be no tears rolling down a mother's face.
Of sadness, there shall be no tracks, no trace.
Birds will chirp love songs.
As lovers welcome the dawn in a warm sleepy embrace.
In another time.
In another place.
There will be no sorrow.
When from out of my dreams...
There is a new tomorrow.

You're A Flame

Love grew a flower.
A perfect rose!
A flower that is you.
So now whenever I'm in despair.
Whenever it seems nobody in the world cares.
Like the stars that beautify that night sky.
You're the reason happy tears fall from my eyes.
The reason my spirits soar throughout the night.
The reason I'm able to find my way,
You're my light...
In the dark of the deepest sea,
You're the beacon guiding me safely ashore.
Indeed, you're heavenly sent.
You're a flame.
I love the way you touch me with your warmth.
With the sweetness of your smile.
Especially at the close of an evening.
When you say good night.
More so at dawn...
When you touch me with the soft freshness of your eyes.
You bring magic to my world.
I swear, even on cold winter night I can't deny,
In the chimney of my life you're the flame.
Shining through the windowpanes of my empty soul.
So generously giving light.
Giving warmth to a lonely heart.
In hollow life I feel resurrected,
Your presence transforms my darkness.
Into a wonderland of brightness.
It's real magic, it's like two magicians working at the same time.

When you whisper hello...
The air I breathe tastes like cotton candy.
That's why I know to the torch of my life,
You're the flame...
The vision...
The very image of every man's dream of a wife.
I pray the heavens have no curfew on you.
There's nothing I wouldn't give or try to become.
In order to stand it, the altar with you.
Blessed with honor to say I do.
Make no mistake about it,
To love you forever is not just a dream.
To be a part of your team.
Indeed, it's the essence of my soul's need.
To some maybe many
I sound insane... Perhaps I am insane.
To believe I can have the heart of an Angel.
Still I feel no shame.
I implore the heavens for mercy.
Because I think about you all the time
When I'm happy.
When I'm in despair and feeling lost.
It's like magic touches my candle...
And you're the flame.

I Wish Every Day...
Could Be Another Yesterday

The memories we made are beautiful.
They're like the stars that give glamor to the night sky.
Whenever I close my eyes,
I watch the many cinemas we made together.
It's no surprise I'm still enchanted by each moment.
Throughout the many years you were the air I breathed.
As each day would begin,
You were the rain my heart and soul bathed in.
Life with you... It was like a story book tale bigger than Cinderella.
Bigger than Romeo and Juliet.
It was even bigger than the love Jack gave to Jill.
Imagine! He ran all the way up a hill to get a pale of water.
You! You brought heaven to earth.
You were the magic that erased all my fears.
Your touch, your smile, your soft whispered hello,
Filled my heart with a waterfall of happy tears.
In lots of ways, you were incredible. Like the rainbows that decorate blue skies.
You were special.
You dazzled me with just a kiss.
More! Never in the nine lives of a cat would I have ever believed.
I would witness the beauty of a sunrise at midnight.
But when you smiled my whole world went from dark to something bright.
As if the dawn was under a blanket of a twinkling constellation.
Being romanced by moonlight.
It was genuine splendor.
It appeared as if the sky was full of diamonds. You were everlastingly beautiful.
The beauty of you still mesmerizes me.
Though today much is my wander.

When Love Came from the Dark

I feel like the little lamb alive without Mary.
I feel lost without you.
My life is like a rose in the midst of winter struggling to stay alive.
It's cold, needing the warmth of a summer sunrise. My heart shivers in pain.
Still I reach for you at night.
I still call out your name.
Sadly, I awake each morning feeling as if I've transitioned
From something sensible to something insane.
Boy! I wish every day…
Could be another yesterday.

The Essence of My Heart's Pleasure

When we first met, I had a good feeling about you.
Since the inception of our relationship,
I've learned nothing but more good stuff about you.
To my heart and soul you've proved to be nothing but a sweet treat every day.
You've allowed me to brisk in the warmth of life.
To feel the true joy of happiness.
You've helped me understand the value of real love.
Unselfishly, you've given me true love.
A love I've searched for all of my life and missed.
You've shown me why even a heartbreak is worth the risk.
In a unique way, you've helped me understand why Mr. Smokey Robinson,
Talked about dancing with his love upon the Milky way.
Why Marvin Gaye said," how sweet it is to be loved by you".
I know I've said it before but I've got to say it again.
I love you! I'm a pure junkie for your love.
You're my drug of choice, and I just can't get enough of you.
You've gotten deep into me.
I feel you in my stomach in my bloodstream.
It's like a sip of strong whiskey warming the whole of me.
I kid you not everything about you excites me.
The way you talk, always wearing a beautiful smile.
The way you walk, especially in jeans real tight.
The way you dance into the night with a subtle seduction.
It's intoxicating, the way your body moves like waves in an ocean.
Coming to shore splashing its kisses up against the rocks of my emotions.
I love being lost in you, you have a heart of gold.
The things you make me feel, the joy you give will never get old.
I swear, everyday with you is Thanksgiving.
Every night is Christmas Eve.
I could easily write a story about you.
But it's something the world would never believe.

You're incredible.
You're worth more than a Pirate's treasure in every way imaginable.
It may sometimes be difficult to believe or for you to understand,
Why I appreciate you.
But do believe I'm happy to have been chosen to be your man.
Honestly, you're my soul's treasure.
You're the essence of my heart's pleasure.

An Impeccable Prize

After all we've been through,
Both heaven and hell.
We're still together, King and Queen.
Two hearts beating stronger than ever.
I cannot say enough about your lovely ways.
I only know it helped me survive many dark days.
The ingredients of life's recipe.
That solidifies the fibers of my spirits and mind.
The soil that nurtures my soul.
The reason it blossoms like the fruits in springtime.
I've been gifted for sure with the likes of you.
Maybe I've even been forgiven for my sins, too.
For even in disguise!
Evil could not be blessed...
With such An Impeccable Prize.

No Lies

Times were tough before I met you.
My dreams were the wishes that I would find you.
For only the master of the constellation of the stars can tell.
That it's because of you.
I have peace in hell.
You're really a dream come true.
You're greater than a prayer to me.
You're like a giant eraser on a chalkboard of misery.
One swipe and my life was changed.
Washed clean as if showered by an avalanche of rain.
I swear, insatiable is my thirst for your touch.
Your kiss and the warmth of your thighs.
Alarm you not...I trust.
For I tell no lies.

Happy Valentine's Day
But it's no fairy tale...

It's truly because of you.
My spirits soar like that of a bird.
With the greatest of ease.
All the time partying in outer space exploring life amongst a twinkle twinkle.
Skipping from star to star.
Dancing on the Milky Way whenever I please.
And each time the heavens blink an eye,
Under the moonlight with prayer I'm on my knees.
Giving thanks for being gifted with you.
Asking to be showered with the wisdom of a child.
That gives peace to a mother's heart and makes her smile.
For with such knowledge though I am a man.
I will hope to implant that which helps you understand,
That that which I am in need of to continue growing strong,
Comes from the cradle of your love.
So know my dear! What Delilah did to Samson,
Will not compare should you leave.
You will have clipped my wings and rendered me weak.
With short foot falls in a jungle,
A spider, even an ant, I will not defeat.
For broken and incomplete like Humpty Dumpty will be my plight.
Although a dark and sad life will not obliterate the memory of you.
For I shall forever hug my one dream come true.
Still, proudly I say please.
Whatever the future may bring, don't ever leave.
For truly it's you that makes my heart swell.
All the time! It's no fairy tale.
So happy Valentine's Day.

Just One!

If I could have but one wish granted,
One dream come true,
Wisdom! I would ask to possess,
So that I could fully express exactly how much I appreciate you.
I would be the man you could forever count on.
In the quiet of your moments,
I would enfold you in arms that are strong.
Erased would be all sadness.
For through you!
Conquered would be the pursuit of happiness.
I can just imagine coming home to you.
The man after dinner helping you with the dishes.
Late night after your bath,
Happily I would rub your feet.
Hold you close and load you up with kisses,
Make love to you in all kinds of positions.
Nothing would be wrong, everything would be right.
We would be our own love story.
Having lots of pillow fights in a sea of candlelight.
It would be a world free of misery.
A private galaxy for just you! Just me.
If I could have just one wish granted.
Just one dream comes true, I'd be a happy man.
With Just One

If Only Tomorrow Would Come

Under the moonlight.
My soul drowns in a sea of sleepless nights.
In awe, tired eyes look upon the beauty of the constellation.
Fingers crossed wishing on shooting stars.
My search for a future,
A promised life with laughter seems lost.
A thousand times I've called tomorrow.
But there's no answer.
Only a cold silence.
Though I have no direction,
I pace counting my footsteps.
My every move is a risk.
Useless, there's no forward progress.
No sight of happiness.
I'm doomed...
My world cannot spin without your kiss.
Still though cursed...
I sip on yesterday's memories to quench my thirst.
To assuage the need for your touch.
I remember years ago when you walked into my heart.
It was simply a moment of splendor.
Today, in each of my dreams, my fantasies,
Though you belong to another, you play an important part in my world.
Thoughts of you resurrect the whole of me.
Something magical happens whenever I think about you.
A beautiful rhapsody resonates within my soul.
It fills me with joy I cannot disguise.
In the shower my vocals are amplified.
It feels like a high school romance.
Visions of you makes my soul, my heart and my spirits really dance.
In the dark of a dungeon,

When Love Came from the Dark

I cherish the moments as if death,
Like a thief under the cover of dark awaits to plifer my next breath.
You are my world.
You are my life.
You are the sole reason...
I would make any sacrifice!
If only tomorrow would come.

Forever Mine

My heart beats to the rhythm of your foot fall.
My soul blossoms under the warmth of your gaze.
The sound of your smile gives me peace.
It makes my spirits swell like bread dough when full of yeast.
You're the air I breathe, the elements of my life.
You're my stars, my sunshine, my moon.
Be it walking to the altar or simply jumping over a broom,
I welcome you to the position as my wife.
For you are the yellow brick road to my happiness.
You're the beauty in my world.
You're the fairy tale in each story told.
Time will only prove that within my heart,
You're forever mine.

Happy Valentine's Day

A box of chocolate candy.
Perhaps something that sparkles suits your fancy.
Or maybe a bouquet of flowers.
Is the sunshine that makes your heart blossom.
But for me...
Your smile, your kiss is the light that erases my gloom.
Your closeness dissipates the chill of cold.
Like blankets your hugs give warm pleasure to my soul.
Eternally grateful I am many times over again,
To have found in you a much needed and desired friend.
Never will I take anything for granted.
Though the way you love greatly energizes me.
It makes me wanna explore your entire planet.
Swim all of your deep seas.
It makes me wanna claim all of your mountains.
Because you really bring out the better man in me.
You make me appreciate life.
You make clear the value of having a good wife
I'm not perfect in the midst of trying times,
I'm just trying to be better.
So will you consider being my valentine.

Happy Mother's Day

It's without doubt,
You're a gift from something sacred.
A gift possessing the beauty of an angel.
You're a miracle amongst stars.
For you're wise in counsel, gentle yet firm and bold.
A Lioness who ensures the safety of her cubs.
The soil of your knowledge and understanding serves you well.
Your garden produces some of the finest of fruits.
You've nurtured a generation from the dark winters of puberty.
To a spring filled with the blossom of adolescent splendor.
One that grew into a beautiful summer of adulthood.
I'm indeed grateful to be the product from your love.
From the warm coolest of your sunshine and rain.
I am also proud that you were chosen to be the rainbow for my sky.
For you allow the innocent to find their way.
Thus, I am blessed with another moment to wish you,
A happy Mother's Day

High School

A dream that came true.
A real Sunday's school morning.
There were no hard times.
Poverty was prevalent...yes!
All around it inundated the land.
Still, I was a happy boy.
In a rush to become a man.
I had a real Cinderella.
A rainbow that decorated my blue skies.
A magic wand that erased all strife.
She was a fantasy that became a major part of my life.
It was just like a song.
It was like a good movie.
When we were young.
When we were in love.
My life was the paragon of happiness.
It exemplified paradise.
At dawn, I awoke simply thankful for another day.
I cannot lie...
For the life of me I cannot deny,
She was the reason happy tears fell from my eyes.
Life was really cool.
Truth to tell...
She was the reason I went to school.
She was like magic...
A girl sought after by wise men, the rich and young fools.
Beautiful and simply stunning.
She captivated hearts with just her looks.
Indeed, I was a happy little camper just being able to carry her books.
I could not control the way she made me blush.
She did something special to me with just a single touch.

Her smile was like the moonlight.
My soul, my heart and my spirits sparkled.
Like a Christmas tree with a thousand lights.
Yes! I broke many rules.
But life was really cool...
In high school.

If Only I Had a Chance

I've seen you smile.
So beautiful! I stood watching you for a while,
I heard your laughter, too.
Pure romance to my heart.
It sounded like a melody from my favorite love song.
Enwrapped in hope.
My soul found cause to stand strong.
My heart was wishful believing dreams of being with someone like you.
Could one day come true.
Much is my wonder...
What would happen if opportunity allowed our hearts to meet?
If the goodness in you caused my heart to play for keeps.
Would you understand the need to be close to you?
A soul's plea...
In an ordinary sense can you picture divine intervention.
Often I wish...
Your heart could hear the spirits of my heart's prayer.
As they parade around you.
In the ways of a simple man.
I speak a truth to you, a truth witnessed by those greater than me.
I pledge my allegiance to loving you.
To make you as happy as I can.
If only I had the chance.

You're The Warrior

The way you smile hello.
I feel a warmth as if your arms are around me.
Your magic, I feel it romancing my soul.
Even in the dark, my sky fills with rainbow beauty.
It rains with a story book wonder.
Where fury tale dreams come true.
You make the sun, the moon and the stars,
In the universe of my heart all come out to play.
You make my spirits blast off in a special way.
Birds even sing at midnight as if it's dawn.
Your touch makes life a lot of fun.
Everything is so perfectly bright and perfect.
Like in a fantasy...
When you're listening to your favorite love song.
In a deck of cards...
you would certainly be the Queen of Hearts.
In the presence of any crowd,
You wear the crown that gives notice to a special someone.
For you're the Warrior!
Forever defeating all of my misery.
The vitamin C that keeps me strong.
Forever and always bringing out that best in me.

Resurrected

I remember the day I met death.
There was a cold emptiness in my heart.
An emptiness as if of blood there was nothing left.
I remember hearing my soul scream out like that of a child in pain.
Fear gripped me tightly.
I pleaded with the heavens to embrace me in their arms but my prayers
Were all in vain.
I was deeply confused. I could feel my spirits losing control,
Though in the midst of their youth they were rapidly growing very old.
As I stood in the chambers of the Dark Prince desperately needing to be brave nothing made sense.
I lost my sunshine, the beauty of a rainbow that decorated my blue sky.
The raindrops that once fell from the clouds were falling from my eyes.
The noise from jingling keys caused panic as giant hands fenden iron shackles to my limbs.
It seemed flames had been ignited inside my body burning it like lava scorches the earth.
A cruel realization gripped the whole of me, vividly I could see I had obviously been cursed.
No one heard my prayers,
As a voice coming from a figure attied in a black role sentenced me to death.
I realized no one else cared that the candle that had given me life had been extinguished. There were no more seasons to life.
Summer, fall and spring for an inexplicable reason had all become winter.
I prayed though it made no sense, I prayed for strength.
I prayed for seventeen long years that I would find tomorrow.
As each morning denied me the warm rays of sunshine and instead bought me sorrow,
Many times I remember my mind was on the verge of going insane.
Often I felt no shame lying on the concrete floor of a dungeon.
I no longer felt the pain as the flames of hell continued to cook the life from

what was left of me.
Often I welcomed death but each night with what seemed to be my last breath I prayed.
I prayed my soul would be forgiven as I fell into a deep sleep.
I dreamed that I had found my lost sunshine.
I dreamed a rainbow dancing across a blue sky had found me.
It was to my amazing surprise when I opened my eyes.
The soul that I thought had been rejected had been resurrected.
I was no longer in prison

A Bachelor No More

I've wished upon all the stars.
I've wished upon everything in the universe.
I've even wished upon everything on planet earth.
Still I'm alone.
In life I've heard patience is a virtue,
And throughout the length of my adolescent years,
I've heeded the counsel of my elders.
So now that I'm in the midst of adulthood,
I ask why my heart is still in so many tears.
Why do the chill of twilight still find my soul quivering from fears.
I pray though I know it's a price Bad Boys must pay.
But must I really endure total darkness another day.
If understanding finds reason to embrace my plight,
Surely you fairy maiden will endeavor to erase my strife.
I implore you to search your heart and write to me.
Let your letters be the sunshine that makes my life blossom.
For my wounds leave my body extremely sore.
Rescue me let not me be a bachelor no more.
Fill the void in my life the most important part.
Let together be our destiny to embrace a fresh start
Let your love be the candle that gives light to my heart.

An Angel Came...
When I Called His Name

I opened my eyes but it felt just like I was dreaming
My life had nose dived, it had crashed.
In the midst of a wilderness I had found myself.
I was in a desert with trees for nothing moved except the heat.
I could feel it crawling on me with the weight of iron chains.
I struggled to focus my thoughts.
I tried to make some sense of my plight but I was lost.
Try as I must, I could not even remember my name.
As my body throbbed with pain the taste of blood filled my mouth.
My soul pursued the earth searching for tracks.
As my spirits scrutinized each branch desperate for signs of life.
A bird, an Ant, a fly or anything.
All grew more strange as I heard the wind whisper a soft melody.
I watched the leaves wave goodbye to the light.
As the darkness waltzed across a foreign land,
I could smell the scent of danger lurking
I fought against the panic though I could feel it watching me.
In the moment I felt sacrilegious, my soul and spirits all screamed.
I prayed in the Lord's name.
Suddenly I was transfixed by a never before seen measure of beauty.
My fears were transfused with warm liquid smiles.
They nourished like manna, and I could feel their presence.
I heard my voice ask who are you.
I am an Angel.
Your heart cried out in my Lord's name.
This is the reason I came.

Summertime

Walking hand 'n hand.
On the beach.
Barefoot in the sand.
It's Summertime.
Being with you Beneath the warm rays of a beautiful sunset.
Soaking in the comforts of a gentle breeze.
Enrich my spirits
It enhances the values of life from zero!
To that of a thousand strings of pearls.
Lucky! Truly blessed I feel.
To be a part of your world
An Evening strolling alone.
Watching mighty waves rollin', Tomblin', Splashing wet kisses against the rocks.
Seagulls soaring above.
Riding the winds searching for treats
In the moment,
The world seems perfect, so complete.
No hate! No prejudice!
Love! Like Hot Dogs, Cotton Candy,
The smell of Grandma' Apple Pie.
Permeates the air.
As do grasshoppers
Kids! Play without worry or a single care.
The moment is paradisiacal...
Magical!...like a Cinderella story.
The beauty of you.
Keeps me feeling like the birthday boy
Each hug, Each kiss, Feels like I've just received another gift.
Yes!...being with you.
Be it Fall or the Winter season.

To my heart, to my soul, To the whole of me,
It's Summertime!

Thinking of You

I heard a whisper in my dream.
I felt a soft touch caress me.
A beautiful fragrance aroused my senses.
I opened my eyes to see no one
Still I knew you were there.
A brief moment, startled I was.
But the blanket of your love comforted me.
I felt imperious like a King very important
Then something moved and a warm breeze touched my face.
Dawn arrived!
I realized again it was you my thoughts embraced.

My Peace My World

In you! I find a fun life.
In you, I find the real American dream.
The true essence of the pursuit of happiness.
When you smile...
I witness a hundred or more reasons,
Why I fell in love with you.
Every time my thoughts land on you.
Every time I look at you.
I witness why sunshine touches my soul.
Even in the dark!
Whenever I'm plagued with a distance that separates us...
A distance that makes my blood rush.
I can see clearly exactly why I miss you so much.
Though when we are apart
Thoughts, visions and dreams of you surge through my heart.
It's ecstasy! An encore of events romances my memories.
For want of you my soul screams.
As if I'm a fish flopping around on dry land
And you're my rivers and streams
My sanity, My peace
The nutrients that keep me strong.
The reasons I'm never weak
live a happy camper, a spirited gentle man.
Because of you!
Day n' night I give thanks to our Lord
For touching me with the rays of his light.
I am grateful for many things.
To the Lord for blessing me with you.
I am forever thankful.

In Just a Day a Lifetime I Live

It's the same chapter.
Each word is a foot step.
Each foot steps a word
The Dawn blinks and yawns.
The Sun rises but it's another storm.
Rudely and roughly imposing and demanding more.
A simple day yet distance the journey.
The road in need of repair is bumpy.
The task is more laborious for naught the moment to capture a breath.
To nourish a torn body to replenish its vigor, its strength.
Energy reserves though drained face yet another mile.
Fueling the storm in a sky of insanity, emotions cloud.
Spirits plummet nose diving like predators.
The Sunset rays nudge you around.
Emitting a moan distress seemingly tracks the ground.
As a weary soul forges toward the twilight.
Clawing to reach the comfort of a familiar sight.
A chamber of emptiness.
Where darkness expels judgment.
Where it blankets an aging pain.
Where it welcomes the beauty of a waterfall.
Where tears have no shame.
Alone I am, In the safe haven of my guardian's embrace, a warm Slumber! An underground railroad to peace.
Twist, turn and sculpture dreams under the cover of moonlight.
In its midst I scout for a glimpse, a smidgen, a mere flicker of tomorrow's light.
But again strangled is hope.
For midnight! Approach another day of yesterday.
To turn the page, To read the next chapter,
Sometimes I feel, It is of my soul I would give.

To alter the next lifetime I live.

You're the Reason!

My nights no longer plague my soul with sleeplessness.
Because of you instead of being strangled by loss,
When I reminisce I breathe fresh air.
I dance with hope once harnessed with despair.
Finally I see an opening at the end of a long tunnel.
You're the light that gave life to my darkness.
The magic wand that granted all my wishes.
You're the magic that makes each moment I live Sweet and delicious like gourmet dishes.
Never could I have asked the heavens for more.
I swear! You're the answer to all my prayers.
Let not it be a secret!
I long to hold you close to feel your warmth.
To quench my thirst with your kisses.
To replenish my weary soul with the joy it's been missin'.
It seems like a lifetime pursuit.
In earnest you're the kind of girl I've been after.
You're the chosen one of my desires.
You're the Special Someone I need to be the keeper of my castle.
That's why you're the target of my passion.
That's why I give thanks to you.
For you're the reason my dream came true.

Giving Thanks!

It's truly amazing.
How even in the midst of a winter storm I can feel your warmth.
How in your absence I can feel your presence.
How the beauty of your smile embellishes the sky of my heart.
Like twinkling stars makes the sky beautiful at night.
In the dark of a moment the thought of you alone gives me light.
It somehow strengthens my weary bones. Though wounded it leaves me feeling Superman strong.
The measure of your love resurrects my hopes. It helps me plant the next foot fall needed to carry on.
I'm certainly blessed that my prayers were answered.
Granted were my wishes and all my dreams came true.
When the Lord allowed me to be a special part of you.
Allowed you to be a part of me.
So nightly! Even sometimes at Dawn I'm down on my knees,
Giving Thanks to our Lord.

Bright Nights... Await me!

I'm as sure as the trees.
In the season of fall awaiting the golden moment To shed their Autumn leaves.
That somewhere within a nocturnal establishment,
Where silhouettes from chimney flames embellish the walls.
I'll find the splendor of its glamor accentuated by only the brightness of you.
A midnight sunrise with the freshness of morning dew.
Pure honey! Dripping like winter icicles.
In the wake of Springtime You're the sweetness in fine peace wine.
The sweetness that bedazzles mankind for miles and miles.
Each time you grace the world with the enchantment of your lovely smile.
Your presence! It's intoxicating and simply breathtaking.
The mere thought of you alone feels my soul with joy.
It turns me completely upside down.
Like a child on Christmas with a room full of toys.
Constantly I'm spinning out of control.
But despair not my dear distance may hold us apart.
Still I swear! Though the Heavens forbid, Only you can dance on the stage floor of my heart.
Only you burn within my soul like the flames of an Olympic torch.
It's miraculous! The way visions of you give me such a rush.
The way I can feel the magic of your touch.
Though It's a mystery.
I'm sure Bright Nights Await Me.

Simply Wonderful

From a tiny seed to a little tender bush You grew strong.
Throughout life's evolutionary process,
The seconds and the minutes with each hour You blossomed.
The winds of time periodically pushed you around.
Still you became a beautiful flower.
In large part because of such...
Through the eyes of my heart you continue to bring lots of joy!
The fervent spirits embodied within my soul stands superman proud.
As moments from the moment crawls upon us.
In the midst of springtime April showers,
Anxious I am to welcome our new addition.
My grandchild's child.
Another branch to grow from our great tree.
Another beautiful part of our family.
Distance may hold us apart but forever is the time I shall be here for you.
Forever long shall be my love's reach.
As I live for the moment to witness your smile.
To listen to the magical melody of your laughter.
To be a part of that which protects you.
To help you continue to grow.
For indeed you are a Wonderful One.

My Only Wish

Sometimes when I look at you.
Your picture or my thoughts just chance upon you,
It really feels like christmas.
The world is simply a huge tree.
Beneath it you're the present heaven sent to me.
It's strange I close my eyes to fathom its mystery.
All to no avail, it's difficult.
More than trying to fathom the mystery of blue skies.
Though still there I do find your smile.
I find a warmth within you soothing to my soul.
It's magical, Somehow in my troubled moments it erases the dark.
Like the Dawn on days in Springtime.
So easily your charms make my heart blossom.
I can sometimes taste you
I can smell your scent in the wind.
For you're the flower.
I'm like the Butterfly stealing your kisses by the hour.
I simply love being in your garden listening to your laughter.
It's the music that makes my spirits dance.
Happy! I feel like Romeo and Juliet did.
Light is my touch though powerful I am when I'm with you.
So come with me! Lie your body upon mine until the morning comes.
Let me love you a thousand times.
For you're the center of all my plans.
I swear! My only wish is to be your man.

A Lonely Grave

In the middle of a nightmare.
I heard my heart scream.
It felt like my flesh was being twisted and torn.
I awoke to the feel of a burning pain.
In fright I looked around.
My search for something familiar was to no avail.
Everything in sight was simply strange.
I waited for a foot step and whispered any sound.
There was nothing I was alone.
I closed my eyes to recall a semblance of something.
Anything but my subconscious deserted me.
Though a Warrior whose physical wounds eventually heal.
My wonder and imagination left me harnessed with worry.
As I greatly fear afflictions to the heart.
My soul requires a special nurturing.
Something from a kindness that can expunge an ugliness.
I know not the message from my dream.
Though I pray entreating the Lord for heaven's mercy.
For the sword of life struck me with a near fatal blow.
I am now lost and confined to a foreign land.
Still your fingertips I long to caress with my fingertips.
Your lips I long to kiss with my lips.
Your heart I long to hold close to my heart.
In prayer I do ask for much.
To be touched again by your lovely ways.
To once again explore your embrace before a lonely grave.

I Really Miss You (Remix)

This ain't no joke it feels like a habit.
The Summer of my life is gone. It's Fall, almost Winter.
Though still I can feel the warmth of you.
The Autumn leaves remind me of your beauty too.
The bright colors somehow enchant my senses.
In its midst I wonder why am I alone.
I wonder where you might be.
In memory as I stroll down narrow trails,
The scent of love in our wilderness is so prevalent.
The Forest seems to read my thoughts.
As cool winds caress them, trees smile.
Life seems so different as I listen in awe.
To the Birds romance our wonderland with love songs.
I crave your company.
As I sit upon the earth at twilight.
I wish for our bodies to be entwined.
Though I invite not the beauty of the twinkling stars.
For I can only extend such an invitation.
To the expiration of the moment that brings tomorrow.
I miss you terribly.
The Dawn that brings us together comes much too slowly.

You Love Me

You say you love me.
But lately I've been having trouble feeling you.
You've got my heart singing the blues.
I can't lie, I just don't know what to do.
So listen to me, It's been too long since you've been home.
I wanna tell you about the way I've been missing you.
All the lonely nights I wanna tell about the hell I'm going through.
You say you love me,
I need to believe it's true.

Nothing Left

When I explored the caves within my soul. I discovered a book of my life. In perusing its contents my eyes touched your name.
There written across my heart in pastel splendor,
I could see images of you in each letter.
I watched as you matured and grew gracefully with time.
You were beautiful like the blossoms in the midst of springtime.
My excitement and curiosity accelerated my exploration.
I wanted to touch you.
I wanted to inhale your fragrance.
I wanted to dance with you.
I wanted to laugh with you.
Strange though, in my book there was only one chapter.
I was harnessed with wonder. Could there be a surprise?
Perhaps we were destined to meet upon my demise.
A confirmation of such would give welcome to death.
For of this earth without you,
There would really be nothing left.

This Song's for You

Every time I think of you.
I can feel a new rhythm in my heart.
I can feel it spinning around and around.
Happy as if rescued from the lost and found.
I can feel it dance every time I speak your name.
I see sparks. I can feel you ease my pains.
I can feel my soul get a fresh jump start.
Still I just don't think I could carry on in this world.
If we ever had to part.
So this song's for you.
For all the lovely things you do.
Cause I'd be lost in this world without you.
No one is more deserving of my praise.
My love shall forever be yours.
I swear even after I'm in my grave.
You took my soul with love, you nourished me.
You submerged me in river waters to purify me.
To let my heart breathe again to strengthen me.
You allowed me to see.
For from my eyes you took a cloth that blinded me.
You let me walk in the path of your light.
You made me feel this world belonged to you and me.
So this song's for you.
Cause when I was lost and down in this world.
You picked me up, you turned me around.
You made me feel like a beautiful pearl.

The World is Hooked on You

Oh Boy! Here I go again.
Dark clouds may make attempts to obscure your beauty.
But at Dawn you're like the sunrise.
Forever are the times you come shining through.
Lots of eyes gaze upon your splendor.
Its mystery simply invites lots of wonder.
Even the Winds like lovers whisper throughout the night.
They sip from the glass of your soul.
Though spill not your secrets.
You're chosen cherished are even your tears drops.
For like the rain you make blossoms all of life.
You brighten the spirits of birds and mankind alike.
Daily as they prance gallantly to procure your favor.
You're legendary in your own time.
The glamor of your legendary words may not accurately sculpture
Still Wise Men and Soothsayers voice their fables.
They tell of your warmth as well as of your wrath
Even when the Sun closes its eyes.
Twilight issues lots of invitations.
Many abandon the arms of their slumber.
To chance their hearts being bedazzled by nocturnal charms.
They hope to be the recipient of your falling star.
To make their wish upon.
For Dawn brings only another field of hope to harvest.
Where many will labor under your watchful eyes again.
So what should I do?
The whole world is Hooked On You.

Heart to Heart

If you would be so kind.
Send me an ear to your heart.
So you can listen to the secrets in my heart.
My journey has been far and wide.
My determination has been endless.
My pursuit has been relentless.
Still thoughts of you continue to crawl.
Like little demons on the floor of my soul
I cannot find you.
I am a King now growing old.
I have been haunted by much in yesteryears.
But I must not perish without the crown to my soul.
I ask that you reach out to me
No matter the distance, wave your magic wand.
Change my nightmares into a bright pleasant reality.
I implore you to not let the cruel chambers of hell.
Continue to taunt me to oppress me.
Let there stand naught to hold us apart.
For my appeal to you in truth is heart to heart.

My Simple Thanks

Life! Once burst with the elegance of pastel beauty.
Suddenly a Wind Storm extinguished the flicker of my flame.
Now I am afraid of the dark I am.
Such as afraid of the Wolf the Lamb.
Be it not for you my light.
Perpetuated would be my existence in fright.
I'm grateful for the white linen of your beneficence.
For when obscured by tragedy's mud,
You wipe clean the lens of my life.
Graciously! You resurrected my hopes.
Now though equipped with an arsenal of words.
I'm lost! Even at the close of the tenth chapter.
I've only discovered the depths of my appreciation.
To express it is a lifetime occupation.
So it is my heart and soul,
In the presence of our Lord I pledge as collateral.
I ask that you accept my simple thanks.
As an installment on a debt larger than life.
For though my dreams were the wishes I would find you.
Forever tough were the times without you.
Yes! a dream come true you certainly are.
Even should today find my life's end.
I would smile knowing in you I had found a friend.
And that you can certainly take to the bank.
So please know the measure of my simple thanks.

Another Bad Dream... That's All!

It was late fall.
In an Anger Management class I scored a 'D' but I still passed.
There were others like me.
I won't lie, I was really sort of happy.
Like a kid with a brand new toy I grew strong.
I was not alone, I was officially a good boy.
I had finally made it.
Excited, I ran all the way home
But upon bursting through the door.
Immediately I knew something was wrong.
My steps were cautioned by tear filled eyes.
As the words explored in my ears Santa's gone.
The world stopped My soul seemed transfixed
No! This could not be true.
It wasn't even December 26th.
But misery's grip tightened as my glance darted under the tree
Clearly there were no gifts for me.
What was I to do?
I wished upon all the twinkling stars.
Then it hit me.
What if Santa didn't know I had passed.
Wow! Maybe he's not too far.
Desperately rushing outside I screamed his name.
In the midst lights lit up many window panes.
To a horrific surprise the police came.
A voice boomed. You! Bad Boy!
My heart sank still it screamed.
I'm not bad! I'm not bad. I passed!
I just want my presents to be proud,
That's all.

Really Missing You

Excitement assails my heart.
Each time my thoughts fall upon you.
I think sometimes my world stops.
To keep me from spinning out of control.
For your cute girly ways with the stuff you got.
Inflates the images of tasty desires.
In the candy store of my heart you're my lollipop.
In all my dreams and fantasies you're my private dancer.
For you're beautiful! You're simply hot to trot.
I can't wait to put my arms around you.
My charm inside of you. To show you exactly what I'm talking about.
When we meet, be it christmas time, summer or spring,
It'll be the season of fall like at Halloween.
You'll be the beauty of the autumn leaves that blanket my ground.
That keeps me wishing I was the wind.
That comes so often and sweeps you around.
For to the eyes of all mankind you really are a treat.
You're the sweet stuff that makes my heart skip a beat.
You're my vitamin!
Daily thoughts of you keeps me strong
Keeps me anxious to return to the candy I left at home.
I long to quench my thirst in the river of your passion.
When I'm alone I envision lots of reasons Why I'm so crazy about you.
So at the moment just know.
I really do miss you.

Because of You!

Life! Whenever it feels like the end
I sit in wonder.
Alone in my cloud.
My thoughts rain down upon you.
In the land of you and me it's like beautiful dreams.
The wings of my imagination spread.
Constantly you're in my head.
My spirits seem to drown in a sea of fantasy romance.
Where on the ocean floor.
We dance and dance and dance.
Like yesterday when we first met.
It gives me tons of great pleasure.
To entertain thoughts about the good old times.
Often I can still feel the softness of your lips brush against mine.
I can still see the beauty within your eyes.
Perhaps somewhat silly of me to say.
But it does help keep me alive and Strong!
Hoping one day I can right what went wrong.
I miss the many wonderful things about you.
The ring of your laughter even some of your little corny jokes seem funny now.
Savor the moment my eyes chanced upon you.
Though given another opportunity I cannot explain what possibly I will do. I just know you're my tomorrow.
The reason my heart is not plagued with sorrow.
The memories from being once loved by you.
Shall forever be the stars that fill my sky each night.
The warmth within my soul from God's candlelight.
The reason I cling to hope.
Today may find me alone!
But it's really because of you I'm still strong.

It's Insane

It's a good man.
Your heart desires to serve.
The good woman I see in you I truly believe it's deserve
So if by chance you can.
Please try to understand I'm not the kind of man.
Trying to embrace another victory.
Though each night my heart sleeps in misery.
I'm not the kind of man that seeks to destroy another's family.
It's just that when you're near me.
It's hard to believe what I'm feeling in my heart.
Many would perhaps label it as some kind of fantasy.
But believe me your presence has a powerful chemistry.
I'm almost afraid to even look into your eyes.
I swear I feel somewhat hypnotized.
My feelings are simply hard to disguise.
Especially with your smile being bright like a rainbow.
Across my heart's blue sky.
Your laughter poisons the purity of my soul with desire.
Making it want to dance real close to you.
Because upon us rest the eyes of society.
I dare not risk being the reason they question your integrity.
I can only hope you try to understand
The magnitude of that of which I am dealing.
There are just so many feelings.
Truly it's getting next to me.
Though I am probably deeply wrong.
In truth I wish not to be right.
To be a part of you I would rather live with the sleepless nights.
I would rather let my heart continue to yell.
I would rather live in the midst of my hell.
I know it's insane!

But to be a part of you I would do anything.

Blessed

When my heart is overborne by a thirst for life.
My Soul reaches for a tall glass of you.
Especially at the close of a long warm day.
Where complaints and failure plagues the moment.
Where nothing of substance comes your way.
Where frustration clouds the world of your judgment.
Where impossible is allowed to stare you in the face.
In the presence of such.
My soul struggles with little demons.
In my heart I feel so distanced from being safe.
I hear my soul scream.
Trying to hold on to some fleeting dream.
So I give thanks that my spirits are able to embrace you.
Thanks! you're Heaven sent with special powers.
To transfuse me with knowledge and strength.
That erases a need to guess,
Whether I've been condemned or truly blessed.

Chocolate

If I could be a box of candy.
I would be Chocolate.
You would really find me handy.
In your coffee I would be the sugar and cream.
I would be the reason you had sweet dreams.
The reason you regarded life as if it was a bundle of joy.
My charms would simply make your heart beam.
The way I would fill your body up with my sweet stuff.
They would make your eyes twinkle like midnight stars.
I'm sure moments spent with you would be beautiful.
I'm sure it would be nothing short of wonderful.
For though you already possess sweetness.
I would simply be your fail safe system.
To ensure the life of your happiness.
If I was your Chocolate.
Your soul would scream yum yum yummy.
Your smiles would all have bright lights.
Your laughter would be everybody's favorite song.
I swear I would really feel like a star.
A Queen's Knight, a chosen one.
Wearing the crown representing your Mr. Goodbar
You could keep me a secret if you like.
You can even gobble me all up in one night
More the wise you can just hold me.
You can let me melt right in your hands.
It'll be a little messy but I'll still be good to you.
Think about it the next time we meet.
Because day or night each kiss will be forever sweet.
Maybe you should just go ahead and sample me.
After all, samples are free.

Dream with Me

It's been a long time
Since I've last laid my eyes on you.
It's been a long time.
Since I've last held you in my arms.
But you've been in my heart and in my soul.
You've been in all my dreams.
And you still mean the world to me.
So dream with me
Dream with me for a moment.
If not for love for old time sake.
I know I don't have the right.
To stake my claim on another man's land
And I'm not trying to break up a happy home.
But you put a fever in my soul.
And I can still feel it burning deep in my heart.
So dream with me.
Just for a moment.
Even though I don't deserve a second chance.
Cause I did you wrong.
I still remember the feeling you gave me.
When you held me tight.
The way you took the darkness in my life and gave it light.
I remember every time You put your arms around me.
How you ensured happiness with the soft sweetness of your kiss.
Yes! It's been a long time.
But I still remember the sweetness of your ways.
As if it was yesterday.
So dream with me.
Dream with me for a moment.
Please! if not for love for old time sake.

And early in the morning when the Sun reaches high up in the sky.
Let's just kiss and say good-bye.
For what I did... I'm sorry!
Remember the music from Al Green's song "Funny how time slips away.
I still remember you.

You're Truly Amazing

You're the star in every man's show.
Whenever you smile, whenever you whisper hello.
It's like Wedding Bell Days in June.
The moments with you are special occasions.
They swell people's hearts with beautiful sensations.
Words of certain may fall short,
In describing the splendor of such situations
But in the eyes of my heart you are truly amazing.

Edward Jordan

Happy Valentine's Day – Happy Anniversary

In the smallest words.
Much about the magic of love is foretold.
Especially about that amidst fairytale fables.
The likes of Jack 'n Jill.
Shakespear's Romeo and Juliet.
The wondrous effects of Cupid's little arrow.
Throughout our yesteryears many were the words used to fill the void of lonely hearts.
Renowned Philosophers and Astrologers.
The likes of many others- all extremely smart.
Played an important part.
still when compared to the measure of happiness.
You've poured into my soul.
Second to none do I find you stand.
Of certain your performance commands many thanks.
As over the years many are the reasons.
You've given my spirits to shed happy tears.
I remember the first time. I saw your face.
I saw the sun rise in your eyes.
In lots of ways you were remarkable too.
As I remember the moon the stars were the gifts.
You gave to my dark.
I remember the first time we kissed.
I felt the earth move.
I felt the wind's whisper caress me.
As the rain washed me clean.
I felt brand new like a wrecked car.
At the end of restoration.
Indeed you were the path to my salvation.
To date I remain forever thankful.

For that which you so generously implanted within my life
Like a good wife.
You erased all traces of sadness.
In a soul once marinating in distress.
Where spirits were broken.
You used love to resurrect hopes.
I cannot possibly repay you for what you continue to give
But while we're apart please know.
The smallest words I love you.
Are the biggest of my heart.

Mistakes, Mistakes

If I could just rewind the clock.
Erase the dark, how wonderful.
There's lots of answers when your soul is in despair.
Sometimes the weight of life forces a body
Into a dark seclusion.
On your knees you whisper special words nobody cares about.
When love walks out the door.
Sometimes every thought and every moment seems like a nightmare.
Sometimes it's even difficult to breathe.
It's natural to entreat the Lord.
When loneliness extinguishes the flame of your candle.
It seems impossible to find your tomorrow in the dark.
It seems only pain romances your heart.
Your imagination runs rampant and it goes on a rampage.
It's like Armageddon.
Angry storm clouds hover in the sky of your mind.
Eventually tiny raindrops fall from your eyes.
You search for blame.
You wonder who could have stolen your forever.
How could you have allowed your life to come to this.
I understand my grief is a product of my own mistakes.
I should have been a better man.
Still I cannot deny.
Your presence is far from being all I miss.
My heart shall forever belong to you.
In all earnest I wish you well.
You were simply the best.
No longer privileged as the recipient of your partnership.
Do leave me feeling shameful.
My remaining days without you will be painful.
Still thoughts of you shall always be my light.

When Love Came from the Dark

As the sound of your voice still rings loud in my soul.
Even the softness of your whisper I hear.
I guess those are the brakes.
When a man makes foolish mistakes.

Thuggin' in the Big House

I thought it was just a nightmare.
Waking up next to people choking in their sleep.
From breathing stale air.
I nearly panicked gettin' off a long dark green bus.
Being greeted by a thousand deadly stares.
I ain't trying to tell a lie.
I thought we took a bad turn.
I thought we landed somewhere in hell.
The smell of death was everywhere.
A hundred million people in the world nobody cares.
About the shit goin' on behind these walls.
People are constantly screaming about rehabilitation.
For the crimes I committed.
Ain't no heat in my heart it feels real cold.
And I ain't crying about the situation.
Just understand I live for retaliation.
It's a wicked life but it's all good.
It's another chapter in your life being slammed down.
I'm still standing tall.
And slam dunkin' is the way I still ball.
It's just my only weapon is a knife
The police every day forever making sure it ain't no peace.
They keep shit goin' on all the time.
Spreading propaganda just to murder unite.
Even with your own kind you are never safe.
At any given moment you can catch another case.
It's like a bad joke, hopes of being free.
You were forced to draw some blood.
Your dreams are gone cause now it's strike three.
Immortalized is your life in a dark distance land full of dirty cops that call you

by a number.
Instead of hollerin' at you like a man.
It feels like forever but it's all in a day.
Dealin' with a bunch of redneck bitches from the hills.
They be hatin' on you being real shitty.
Just because you gotta standing reputation from a big city.
But I ain't trippin' I'm really lovin' the shit.
Cause I'm still really thuggin' n' shit.
So holla at me.
Sucka's do a bunch of dumb shit then slam the door.
Death to you is what I feel.
Until I get even on the score.
Cause I pledge allegiance to the game.
You can believe in the shit that I bring.
It ain't questions, we're really full of pain.
My moves ain't got a damn thing to do with no fame.
Take a peek if you can't tell.
My plan is to send your ass straight to hell.
Maybe to you the move is something new.
But to me and the crew we are with the business.
And a trail of blood is our only witness.
It's a bunch of people runnin' around cussin'.
But I'm having fun in the big house.
I'm drinkin' wine but I'm still gettin' the job done
Cause I'm still thuggin'.
Thou shall not kill is what they said.
And We live by it as long as your body is already dead.

In the Ghetto Nothing was Ever Promised

If I could have foreseen the storm.
If somebody had only told me.
Life would be full of death, destruction and harm.
Perhaps over my door.
I could have had the blood of the Lamb
Perhaps I could have been wise in my ways.
Perhaps I could have prepared like a brave soldier would do.
Perhaps I could have become a mighty Knight.
A Prince or even a King.
Perhaps I could have made a stand amongst great men.
Men that knew honor loyalty and what it means.
Perhaps my foot fall would have left tracks of diligence.
Tracks similar to those from men in possession of wisdom.
Men of whom possess knowledge of many things.
Tracks from men that fought with a conscientious heart.
Men of whose association others are happy to proclaim.
But nothing was ever promised.
The storm raged on.
Bright flashes of lightning blinded me.
As thunder boomed its blast deafening me.
I was lost.
Though later discovered in a dark forest.
Strange eyes watched over me.
Everything I touched seemed so peculiar
My heart's fears gave cause to long for something familiar.
In answer to my prayers the storm passed.
Though leaving me in the midst of a sudden quietness.
There was hope I would find my way through the wilderness.
Though still nothing was promised.

Let me Love You

You're really someone very special.
To my heart! You're like a diamond amongst precious stones.
A twinkling star in God's galaxy.
When I look at you my everything spins around.
Until I'm weak instead of strong.
Though conscious often I feel hypnotized by your charms.
I believe not in love at first sight
Still I stand needing to feel you in my arms.
Though I stand proud and strong as a man.
I also stand helplessly needing you to take a chance.
So with my heart in my hands I implore you.
Just let me love you one day at a time.
I swear each year you'll be my valentine.
I'll always be there for you even as the seasons change.
For you're the heat in my winter fires.
You're the light in my dark that sees me through.
I just wanna be a special part of you.
I wanna be your man.
I wanna be the lucky one at the altar that says I do.
I believe you're the girl meant for me.
If not I wouldn't make another choice.
As I believe we'll have a Silver Anniversary.
I know together we can find our way through the years.
Just be the one.
That allows my heart to beat for two.
Just let me love you.

Being Fast

He was tall and rugged in his ways.
Maybe a little more.
I could feel something special in his hands.
Though I couldn't quite completely figure him out.
I knew it was a man.
Loneliness had my heart and his touch.
I wanted it to last.
Funny! He knew I was making a pass.
When I asked him to take me home.
Still he turned and smiled.
And as he took another sip from his glass.
He said I thought you'd never ask.
That's when I knew being fast couldn't be a sin.
Because being fast is the thing that helped me win
Being fast some say it's a shame.
But being fast is the thing that erased all my pains.
My Mama always said I was too fast.
She said my ways would only get me labeled as some trash.
She said she'd never be able to be proud of me.
Because the talk in town would fill her heart with misery.
But it's okay.
Cause I know my Mama loved me in her own stubborn way.
I just wish she was here to see the day.
I landed in the arms of a good man.
To see the day my life found joy
The day I turned out to be a decent toy.
The years have since come and passed.
There's been lots of ups and downs.
Though still he incessantly assures me of my place.
A place that strengthens my faith each morning I awake.
With that man snoring in my face.

Old Fashion Cowboy

I'm just an Old Fashion Cowboy.
In the city missing my country girl.
She's somewhere way out on the prairie.
Riding horses with them short jeans on.
Cause way out there on the prairie.
Where year round the grass grows really tall.
We don't have any worries.
The cattle graze there all day long.
We're up and at it every morning.
Before the sunrise, working hard until the job is done.
Then just before suppertime in early even.
When the sun goes down we sit around.
Telling tales and lots of stories while drinking a beer or two.
Sometimes clowning around pushing n' joking.
Laughing hard and slapping hands.
But never do we try to put another down.
Spreading loose gossip around the town.
We practice being real neighbors.
Cause we take great pride in spreading southern hospitality
So if you understand my story my friend.
And I hope you will so you will understand.
The reason I'm sitting here all alone.
I'm just an Old Fashion Cowboy.
In the city missing my country girl.
I know she's somewhere way out on the prairie.
Riding horses with them short jeans on.
C'mon now y'all know Daisy Dukes.
Back home we don't have any problems.
Playing with girls with short jeans on.
We don't have any worries.
So I hope you understand.

Edward Jordan

I'm just an Old Fashion Cowboy.
In the city missing my country girl.

Moments with You

Just a little bit of lovin' Early in the mornin' will do!
No hold it! I need twenty—four seven.
So bring it! It's guaranteed when we take a break.
you'll swear it's heaven.
You'll know morning, noon, evening and night.
Anytime I touch you is right.
Evening during the day you'll see stars.
Regardless of the weather, fog, clear skies, rain or snow.
You'll be forever the star of the show.
You may not know exactly what you're feelin'.
But with excitement and joy your body will be reelin'.
none stop from bottom to top.
Like a bowl of Kellogg's rice krispies.
You'll be my Snap Crackle and Pop.
Imagine being too high to die.
Overdosed on a feeling' confused without knowing why.
Your body raped by pleasure.
Unable to believe what's presented to your naked eye.
Though a cloud of raindrops fills your soul.
You're unable to cry.
You're enslaved by Love—Mageddon. ...
It's a war between joy and pain.
You have no choice, no direction, no voice.
Blinded by the light.
You spent like a Honeybee frustrated by an artificial smell.
Still like chocolate candy you're simply sweet.
It's easy to tell
Your love forever shall I cherish.
Even should it lead to the gates of hell.
In the deep sea of your love.
I lose sight of both friends and family. As I watch the land recede from my

reach.
I deeply crave just a little bit of lovin'.
I crave the golden moments that find you and me entangled in bliss.
The moments that allow my soul to have its fill.
Of your touch, your hug, your kiss.
The moments where dreams come true.

Happy Birthday

In a calendar year once,
Privileged we are with divine opportunity.
Opportunity to commemorate one of God's creations.
Therewith though harness with abounding thanks.
Your heart fills with joy.
A pristine appreciation.
Spirits embellished with pastel dreams come true.
Soar! Extinguished candle lights ignite clouds of well Wishers.
For the likes of you.
Tumultuous blessings fall like raindrops.
From the tear-strained voices of those dearly beloved.
The atmosphere of sudden inundated with music.
Finds laughter in the eyes where tears used to be.
A beautiful cadence from the chirp chirp of birds.
Permeates the air like oven baked apple pie.
I wish I could still the moment.
I wish every day you could blow out candles.
Wow! My heart screams with excitement.
So do jump up and down and smile.
It's your birthday.
Love,

Yours

To the sunshine of my world
I pray your heart has permanent reservations for me
As my plan is to fill your soul with joy.
To fill you with all that helps sustain life for an eternity.
To spend a lifetime just loving you.
To raise a large family.
I want you to know what I find.
Whenever I look at you.
For you're something much above special.
To my heart, to my soul, my life.
You're the beauty in the colors of my private rainbow.
In all my wishes my dreams.
You're the star of the show.
I swear! The thought of you alone makes my heart swell.
As if it's full of yeast.
It feels magical
It makes my spirits soar.
If being a part of you has anything at all to do with life's final exam,
I'm sure somewhere way up there beyond the heavens and the stars,
I've gotta have the highest score.
For greater than the value of a master's degree, PhD,
In many ways I find you are.
You're wise, you're super smart.
I have no shame, only joy.
Letting the world know you're the ruler of my heart.
So please believe in every way God meant for man and woman to be.
I'm Yours.

When Love Came from the Dark

Though Imprisoned 'You Made Me Whole'

Sad! Truly broken,
Lost in the shadows walking alone.
The whole of me...Confused.
The Judge had said life.
What did it mean?
At the moment nothing made sense.
The words struck like a giant hammer smashing glass.
I felt shattered.
I couldn't understand.
I was blinded.
I couldn't see.
What it was gonna take to feel whole again.
For like a tiny pebble at the bottom of a deep sea.
My soul was submerged into the deep of dark.
My body was completely depleted of strength, I was weak.
Worse! I didn't even know where to start. I felt desperate.
Trial! The journey had been long and hard.
It left me breathless.
I felt bewitched. My life! I felt somebody had cruelly hit an off switch.
There was no light.
There was only the Moon to guide me.
To protect me from the dangers of the night.
I walked on and with each step.
Tears!...like giant waterfalls fell from my heart.
On my knee, I prayed!
Dawn found me cold Trembling.
But I remember your touch.
I remember the way you stirred me. The way you warmed me with the blanket of your sunshine.
So well I remember you.
The sweetness of your rescue, I remember, too.

How you gave my soul a beautiful melody.
I knew the moment you touched my life.
I knew forever, You'd play an important part.
Though my story may go forever untold.
Indeed! you 'My Lord' made me whole.
You resurrected my hope and my spirits.
You gave me life, though I sit imprisoned.
You've set me free.
How Thankful! For you I am.

Just Because

Just because you're in hell.
Doesn't mean you must behave like a devil.
True! Being a resident makes you vulnerable to its inhabitants.
Your interaction with them makes you a greater target.
to their envy and jealousy should you abstain from their activities.
Still you should remember the reward benefit derived therefrom,
comes with consequent punishment and pain.
Be of the wise seek not to possess anything while in hell.
Remember too reward for being there is only suffering.
Strife, stress and struggling are hell's currency.
Departure requires you to be oblivious to...
Not in possession of its currency.
So be victorious!
Your knowledge and your belief to gain success need not be an illusion.
Practice admonishment using faith.
Absent excellent acts or an equivalent yields subquality fruit.
The spoiled rotten fruit readily available in hell.
Some are coveted but only good fruit will be beneficial to you.
Apply yourself as would a man in an ocean with no sight of land.
You'll eventually escape the pains of hell.

No Hold it!

I need twenty-four seven.
So bring it!
It's guaranteed when we take a break.
You'll swear it's heaven.
you'll know morning' noon, evening and night,
Anytime I touch you is right.
Evening during the day you'll see stars.
Regardless of the weather, fog, clear skies, rain or snow.
you'll forever be the star of the show.
You may not know exactly what you're feelin'
But with excitement and joy your body will be reelin',
None stop from bottom to top.
Like a bowl of Kellogg's rice krispies.
You'll be my Snap Crackle and Pop.
Imagine being too high to die.
Overdosed on a feeling' confused without knowing why.
Your body raped by pleasure
Unable to believe what's presented to your naked eye.
Though a cloud or raindrops fills your soul,
You're unable to cry.
You're enslaved by Love-Mageddon. It's a war between joy and pain.
You have no choice, no direction, no voice.
Blinded by the light.
You're spent like a Honeybee frustrated by an artificial smell.
Still like chocolate candy you're simply sweet.
It's easy to tell.
Your love forever shall I cherish.
Even should it lead to the gates of hell.
In the deep sea of your world.
It's so beautiful,
I lose sight of friends and family.

When Love Came from the Dark

As I watch the land recede from my reach.
I deeply crave just a little bit of lovin'.
I crave the golden moments that find you and me entangled in bliss.
The moments that allow my soul to have its fill,
Of your touch, your hug, your kiss.
The moments where dreams come true.
Are the moments with you.
Love.

My One Desire

You left your fingerprints on my heart.
During the Spring season of your adolescent years.
It was really easy to tell.
You would grow to be somebody smart.
Somebody exceptionally, somebody really remarkable.
Somebody inside n' out is simply beautiful.
Wishful my heart grows.
To quench my thirst with the likes of you.
To sip on your smile, your hugs and kisses.
I swear dreams of you continue to caress my soul.
Now that you're all grown up.
I wonder how far you will travel.
Where will you come?
I wonder if tomorrow will find you available.
To say welcome home.
Perhaps I do not have the right.
To brisk in the warmth of your starlight.
Still I cannot change the gospel.
I cannot change my wish to be a part of you.
Right or wrong I cannot alter my one desire.
For of my candle you are the fire.
My light!

Loving You

Many times I've asked myself what I would do.
How could I breathe without you?
God's reason for blessing me with you.
I cannot fathom.
A Bad Boy for some years I've been.
But obviously there are other reasons.
The Heavens are forgiving me for my sins.
So daily I struggle to learn many things.
Things that help sustain love through any storm.
Things that help keep possession of respect.
Whenever my eyes chance upon you.
It's like reading about a beautiful wonderland.
It's a real fairy tale, in you I see divine love.
The kind of treasure in a woman all men dream of.
So I pray for the possession of the things.
That allows me to show the depths of my appreciation.
Things that make me worthy of your heart's invitation
I hope forever will be the time you find a good cause.
To unite with me in spirit, mind in body and soul.
I pray you continue to find a good cause.
To join hands and celebrate our days as we grow old.
I truly value you.
You're worth more than your weight in gold.
I swear loving you is really a pleasure.

Don't Ever Leave

There's no such thing as love at first sight.
Love must by blind.
The moment my eyes chanced upon you from the very start.
I felt Cupid's little arrow penetrate my heart.
Now whenever I look into the mirror I see laughter in the eyes where tears used to be.
There's joy within my soul.
Where pain used to live.
My heart is now sunshiny and blue.
The skies in the presence of the Heavens are rainbow decorated.
Truth must be told.
It's all because you.
All became a soft warm whisper.
That said hello to me.
Your lips touched me with sweetness.
All became infected with an insurmountable measure of happiness.
A sweetness that was unadulterated
When I first met you.
I was heartbroken, shipwrecked.
In my life there was no happily ever after.
Through sheer desperation I somehow managed to disguise my feelings with laughter.
But night was a nightmare.
While wishing upon the shooting stars that beautify the sky.
My soul under the cover of darkness would silently cry.
Love no longer by my side.
My tears would grow into rivers of sorrow.
Pain would seize my soul with promises of no tomorrow.
As the pains grew I contemplated suicide.
The fear of damnation kept me from pulling the trigger.
my heart and soul screamed in protest.

When Love Came from the Dark

Voicing questions.
How could life in Hell be worse?
I had no answers.
Indeed, I was cursed.
Before you walked into my life.
To smile was difficult.
Life was cold!
Summer mornings were like late night winter storms.
There was always a chill in the air.
Even in Springtime.
I prayed! I would one day find somebody that cared.
Somebody whose heart would talk to my heart.
Somebody whose spirits would hold hands with my spirits.
Somebody whose soul would embrace a like desire.
To grow old with my soul.
When I found you.
When you found me
When we became one.
It may or may not have been love at first sight.
But every moment with you has been a Springtime of joy.
A joy that continues to grow into a warm Summer's love.
So please! Don't ever leave.

My Little Friend

I live for the twilight
My heart blossoms like flowers in Springtime.
In the midst of the night.
As I search the sky for my special little friend.
The Star I made a wish upon.
The Star that twinkle twinkled and my lonely days were gone.
All my empty hours filled with the sweet taste of you.
It's remarkable each time I tilt my glass.
To sip on another thought of you.
I witness another miracle: Fairy tales come true.
I taste Thanksgiving even in the month of June.
All that I imagine seems to materialize.
It's like within you I found answers to my prayers.
It's really so cool.
There will never be an end to my gratitude.
My appreciation for my little friend.
Who made come true all of my dreams.
Making me and you a lifetime team.

Moments

I spent a moment as a child.
Trying to find my way in the dark.
I spent a moment growing up
Trying to understand the silly games lots of kids play in the park.
I spent a moment trying to learn things.
That was supposed to make you smart.
I spent a moment thinking about things.
Mama said it could really break my heart.
Now that I'm a man.
I'm happy for the moments of my past.
They help me see the happiness within you.
I believe it might really last.
Since the moments spent with you.
Paint the memories, the wishes and the dreams come true.
That I see, feel and touch each time I make love to you.
Each time you smile with starlight beautiful eyes
I cannot lie, I come unglued inside.
As if a kid again playing with his favorite toy.
The moments spent with you.
Simply fills my heart with joy.

Missing You

Imprisoned.
The eyes of my heart long to chance upon you.
You're the freedom I miss.
You're the reason my soul pleads.
Like a fish on dry land.
For you're the water I need.
To quench a deep rooted loneliness.
To cleanse sadness.
To re-purify a soiled happiness.
I long for the warmth of your open arms
A Forest where your skilled warrior enjoys being lost.
A haven where sleep brings me peace.
As I breathe in real deep.
The sweet fragrance exuding from the mountains of your twin peaks.
The music of your little giggle I miss too.
The way you romance me for hours and hours.
Like Bumblebees in the springtime romance beautiful flowers.
But in all earnest thoughts of you.
Do keep the sky of my soul sunshiny and blue.
Still when we're apart.
I find myself really missing you.

Always There

Once soaring through the air
Like a bird at dawn my heart would sing.
So rich and warm was life
As if touched by a magic wand.
I could hardly believe it.
My dream was so near.
I could reach out and touch it.
Every day was simply full of fun games.
A grasshopper, I was in the midst of summer's life.
Until a Winter Storm came.
Until suddenly love's thunder exploded in my brain.
Until the Masters of Sin demanded a just recompense.
Therewith imprisoning the whole of my existence.
My world stopped a voice from deep within screamed.
As the lights of hope flapped its wings.
Someone had pulled the plug.
Everything in my Universe suddenly grew dark.
Then I made a long distance call person to person.
Straight from my heart.
Miraculously in an instant a new life was delivered.
As if I had been baptized in a holy river.
Though forbidden I swear.
I knew you were always there.

Life Would Be Complete

Sometimes, I wish I could fly.
Like an Eagle, Soar across the sky.
I wish I could tell you about these things I dream.
It's not a lie.
I wish I could hold you close.
Sip on the beauty I find in your eyes.
When I think about you.
There's so many things.
I wish I had the power to make it come true.
When I think about the things I've ever wanted most in life.
There you are at the forefront.
In the eyes of my heart.
Bright! Beautiful like the stars in the night.
Standing proud exemplifying confidence.
The kind of woman I'd like to engage to procreate life.
To become my wife.
Often, I think about you.
In the way that makes lonely arms hug pillows tight.
Endless is the time you enchant me.
Even from a great distance.
I dream! Spiritually, you give me fever.
You give me that kind of love...I just can't explain.
But every time you hug me, Every time you kiss me.
I can feel your passion crawling through my veins.
I understand the warmth of treasured moments may not last forever.
Still, you make me want to do it again and again.
You give hope.... You keep my heart wishing.
Praying The Dawn finds us in each other's arms.
Breathless! in the safe haven of slumber.
Sheathed from the world's harm.
As the Sunrise beatifies the sky.

When Love Came from the Dark

Its rays creeped through window panes.
Decimating the cold.
To give warm comfort to our soul
I wish I could hear your voice.
Listen to your heartbeat tell me secrets.
I swear! life would be complete.
If you! I could really meet.

Jazz

The sound of beauty.
A rhythm that grips your soul.
Enchants your spirits.
Romances your heart.
Under the warmth of Sunlight.
In the dark.
Beneath the glamor of starlight.
Jazz! Speaks to the world.
Even to those who cannot comprehend it.
Its magnetism challenges their Will.
Draws the spirits to it.
It's somewhat synonymous with evil.
The way it gives promise to your soul.
In a moment's notice.
It's capable of transforming a body feeling worn.
Somewhat dejected and old.
To something young and vibrant.
In lots of cases, consciously!
It fills you with an unadulterated excitement.
As if Heaven sent.
You experience an insurmountable measure of exuberance.
A magic that purges the body of stress.
Dark anxiety...
It emancipates your imagination.
Allowing it to spread its wings.
Soar throughout the galaxy.
Free of curse!
To courageously explore the universe.
Jazz! its comprehension!
Could indeed juxtapose the antidote to the world's oppression.
The Tree of Music has many branches.

All speak its universal language.
Though by preference rather first or last,
I chose JAZZ!

Happy Birthday

I missed your birthday.
The golden opportunity is celebrated once a year.
Truth! It broke my heart.
It left my soul in big tears.
I thought about waiting.
I thought about how to recreate your precious moment.
What will I do with all the missed cheers?
I hope you understand what my heart is trying to say.
you're such a good person.
So though late, please accept my belated greeting.
Happy Birthday.

Another Wonder

Each day.
Each night.
Whenever we kiss.
Whenever you press your body against mine.
Whenever you just hug me.
Inside my heart.
Something warm and beautiful explodes.
In every imaginable way.
It's climatic.
It feels like fireworks.
Like the excitement from a special occasion.
Something lights up my soul.
I swear! my spirits dance.
As the midnight constellation of stars
Magically transforms into rainbow decorated blue skies.
It's as if the Heavens opened its doors.
Just as the song said, "You've got that whip appeal".
Nothing is better than being close to you.
Inhaling your perfumed scented hair.
Feeling the warm fingers of your passion caress my soul.
Lucky! I'm truly blessed.
My words may fall short of expressing the true measure of my thanks for God's gift.
To have someone like you Love me.
It's incredulous, It's more!
Much more than I can ever describe.
Still it's the sum total of my happiness.
The only things life offers I would miss.
If ever my demise became the reason Dawn failed to bless my soul with another Sunrise.
I would miss the beauty I find.

When gazing into your eyes.
The sugar from your kiss.
That sweetens my morning coffee.
The heat from your passion, your Love.
Indeed! It's Another Wonder.

Good Girl vs. Bad Boy

What if up was down.
Down was up
What if the Sunrise appeared at midnight.
The Moon rose at Dawn.
Opposites are said to attract.
So maybe somehow broken hearts.
Can somehow become happy hearts.
Bitter feelings stemming from dark moments.
Culminating into hate.
Can somehow become touched by love again.
I struggle to find answers.
Rest!... evades me.
Sleep brings only night sweats.
Since you left, I've been pounding my head against the wall.
Asking! Questioning with every breath.
The logic of the Sages.
Still there's nothing.
Excluding the pains that bring big tears to my eyes.
The constant flow of unanswered questions.
Ringing within my soul like church bells on Sunday morning.
Continues to ask why
Why! can't forgiveness find its way into your heart.
The whole of me screams.
A thousand times I'm sorry for the wrong I've done.
At each Sunrise persecution seems my only friend.
My indiscretions haunt me.
Shame suffocates my soul.
My heartbeat slows.
It cannot breathe.
Please! I implore you to shower me with your mercy.
Condemn me not for life.

A moment of weakness found me.
Indeed my world is abound with regret.
To the Heavens, I swear a truth.
It is only you I love.
My opposite! My Joy!
A good Girl vs. a Bad Boy.

The Weekend

Long are the days.
As I count the moments.
That eventually brings the weekend.
Excitement flows through my veins.
Like waters flowing through riverbeds and streams.
You! a welcome friend.
In another life perhaps much much more.
Decorate the seconds,
The minutes with glamor and pure splendor.
Wishfulness stands in my heart.
As the beauty of you ignites embers of desire into raging flames.
My touch, Your kiss, Our embrace.
Though forbidden by universal law.
The eyes of my admiration fill with warm wonder.
When you smile
When you whisper your soft good morning hello.
Magically You erase the dark in my soul.
Your kindness awakens distant dreams.
Dreams that once foretold Fables,
Leading me to believe I would one day have an Angel on my team.
To covet the Queen of another.
In all earnestness be not my heart's intent.
Though I cannot exclude the truth.
Happily! I would give chase if ever chance availed itself.
Henceforth, I shall forever appreciate the joy you bring.
Throughout all seasons Winter, Summer, Fall and Spring,
As a Friend! I shall forever cherish you.
Thankfully the Heavens found reason to let the beauty of you grace my life. A beauty that transcends a tortured Soul from the dark lagoon of hell.
To the bright splendor of another wonderful Weekend.
Thank You!

Let Me Shake You Down!

The song says.
Girl! I wanna shake you down.
What you need to know with me.
It's not just in the dark.
Between the sheets In the midnight hours.
I wanna get with you.
It's all the time.
My love doesn't have an off switch.
The flight with me is non-stop.
You travel first class. Around the clock.
I make dreams come true.
It's like being bathed in a tub of pleasure.
All night! you scream a lot.
It's no lie.
I know exactly how to tickle your little spot.
Shake you up Make you moan.
At breakfast, lunch and happy hour.
It's yum! yum! yum! when you are in my world.
I'll treat your body like a Hostess cupcake.
When it comes to love.
I'll lick your wrapper and eat all your crumbs.
Make no mistake.
When I touch your thighs,
Rub your feet,
Kiss the teardrops from your eyes,
You'll know for sure, I've got more than the Midas touch.
I've been endowed with the wisdom of the wise.
So C'mon! take a chance.
Let me be your fantasy.
Let me shake you down.
Let me hold you close.

When Love Came from the Dark

Let me kiss your body all over.
I swear! I won't let you down.

I'm Saying Please...

I've spent lots of time.
Many nights drinking and partying.
Trying to get you off my mind.
I've tried a million things just trying to ease the pain.
I've reached the conclusion.
Maybe I'm cursed.
Because nothing! Absolutely nothing seems to work.
My whole world has been colored blue.
Since the moment I lost you.
All I seem to do day-in and day-out.
I sit around in the dark.
Crying a river may be an ocean of tears.
Drinking cheap liquor.
Trying to mend a broken heart.
The world seems not so kind.
When you're trying to get that special one.
That broke your heart off your mind.
It's hard!
There never seems to be an answer for me.
Not even from the Lord.
Friends all say keep your head up.
Even though the whole damn world knows.
It's only a fantasy.
When a man imprisoned in his own home can stand up on his own.
Especially, when the best part of his world is gone.
Desperate! I've made attempts to be with another.
I've even tried saying I do!
Standing at the altar I closed my eyes for a moment, worse!
I called out your name.
I felt totally ashamed.
Tears filled my heart.

When Love Came from the Dark

As she screamed out in pain I realized.
That no matter what I do.
Everything would forever remind me of you.
I wish we could start all over again.
I wish you'd C'mon back home.
If for no other reason than to be a friend.
Anything that lets me be close to you again.
I am saying please!
These walls in my room are tired of me and my tears.
More! my heart is overdue for reasons to cheer.
So please C'mon home.
People say be strong, but how can a man be strong?
When his strength walked out and left him alone.
How can he hold his head up high?
When tears keep falling from his eyes.
How can he even go outside?
Unless it's in the rain so the tears he can hide.
I wish I could just say I'm sorry.
I'm sorry for the things I said.
I'm sorry for the thing I did.
I must have been out of my head.
Still, I know it was wrong.
I don't deserve a second chance.
But I am asking you to C'mon home.
Let me live again.
Let me be your man.
Yes! I'm saying please.

Hooked on You

Daily! I sit staring at a picture.
A beautiful picture.
That hangs on the walls of my heart.
Your silver smile gives me lots of happy thoughts about you.
I swear, you make me feel so close to my dreams.
They have to come true.
You make me feel like the luckiest man to ever live.
Cause all the love one man could possibly get honey you really give.
You bring out the best in me.
There's nothing to be a shame about.
With you There's nothing to lie about.
You're the one I'm crazy for.
Like Smokey said, "You've really got a hold on me",
And every day I love you more and more.
Sometimes when I look at your picture I'm so turned on.
I have to move around.
I actually start jumpin' up 'n down.
I find myself so excited.
In lots of ways you astound me.
Especially, When you've got your arms around me.
Or when I'm chasing you in a fantasy.
When you kiss me I feel all my prayers answered.
When you hug me I feel all my wishes granted.
Even my darkest moments are filled with skies shiny and blue.
That's why I know I'm hooked on you.
You're my guiding light.
My ship won't sail without you.

When the Storm Comes...

We shall join!
For if you be the sugar.
I shall ask to be the rain.
That melts your heart.
The Accomplice that brings you flowers.
Just to steal your kisses in the dark.
I would even ask to be the spoon that dips into your bowl.
To sweeten the bitter coffee of a tired and beaten soul.
For I am absolutely sure!
The quality of your product would erase all my gloom.
Bring me lots of luck!
To accomplish in one life all that I must.
By giving me the energy from nutrients that even God can trust.
If you're the sugar I believe you to be.
Surely! The spirits of heaven will embrace both you and me.
For all would be said and done.
When the storm comes.

This poem is inspired by Ms. C. Davis, Law Library Supervisor High Desert. One day it started to rain. I said "Look, it's raining!" Ms. Davis, looking somewhat troubled, whispered her words. "I'm gonna be in trouble". I asked her why. Ms. Davis said with a smile, " You know sugar melts when it gets wet". It still warms me inside when I think about the moment. I do really hope you guys enjoy this poem. I hope there's somebody that will be your 'Sugar' When the Storm Comes.

Pretty Girl I Need your Attention

I have a vision.
I see you strolling down the street.
Alone dressed real nice and looking real sweet.
Being a Bad Boy!
I wonder if I could ever be blessed with such a toy.
Because my dreams don't include being alone.
Though I break man's law I still dream of a happy home.
I dream of a woman of substance, someone just like you.
It's perhaps thought to be quite daring of a simple man.
Though perhaps suitable since I too believe in commitment.
I'm strong with shoulders you can really lean on.
So I implore you to take a closer look.
Let consideration change the things I've mentioned.
You never know it just might captivate your attention.
Plus you have absolutely nothing to lose.
So C'mon dance with me.
What I see in you are the things I've heard about you. I'm certain they're infested with truth.
That's why I've got my fingers really crossed.
Hoping for the opportunity to center my plans around you.
Maybe even get lucky and be able to help you raise a child.
Then every time I walk into your home.
I would get two beautiful smiles
Just think loved twice in a wicked world.
I really do pray!
The Lord bless me with a pretty girl.

I Wonder

They say it's a man's world.
But I wonder.
How do you so easily control my heart?
How does your smile so easily interrogate my thoughts?
How do you so easily creep into my sleep?
How do you make my spirits dance when my soul weeps?
How do you make me crave the taste of you?
I even wonder about the reason to change the world.
Since it's you that makes all of my dreams come true.
There's something very powerful about what God has made.
For I know of nothing else possessing the power,
To make me welcome being a slave.
But here I stand strong, vibrant and happy to be your man.
Patiently awaiting your wish and every command.

My Kind of Rain

In the midst of the storm.
When we touch.
When we kiss.
When we hug.
When we warm the midnight with our love.
I feel all the raindrops of your passion. It feels like a mountain waterfall washing over me.
Its heat sort of tickles like little tiny fingers.
It crawls inside my soul constantly stimulating me. Simply refreshing is your presence alone.
In my weakest moments you're my dawn, my morning dew.
You keep my soul and my spirits fresh.
You keep me strong.
Daily you keep me searching for ways to strengthen the foundation of our home.
Never would I ever take you for granted.
For a loss I could never stand it.
You're the reason I'm sound of mind.
The reason love songs, my heart sings. When life has simply driven many others insane.
You're simply the reason my soul is free of pain.
The reason the lands of my life are never Sallow.
Because you're my kind of rain.

Happy Valentine's Day

In the midst of my raging rivers.
Quiet moments dance.
It's all because of you.
Sunny days brisk in the middle of my storm.
In troubled times I feel the lights of your love.
Romance and charm the evils of my dark.
When it comes to my happiness,
Forever seems like the time you play an important part.
And forever is the time I shall carry you in my heart.
You never fail me, you never let me down.
Your love allows me to walk without fear.
Its presence makes me feel useful.
I feel strong as if invigorated by the touch of an Angel.
Even in the midst of sad times I shed happy tears.
Its magic seems to make me grow younger in spirit.
Daily with the pasting of each wonderful year.
In sum I can never lay claim to hard times.
Since birth! I've been blessed with a true valentine...You

My Only Drug

You're the best thing in my life.
You're the reason for my existence.
Second to none there not shall you ever stand.
You're greater than the beat of my heart.
You're simply important, you're so necessary.
At the Wake of Dawn til twilight I search for you.
To find the flower that gives beauty to my sights.
I breathe deep to track your fragrance.
In all my dreams I count on you to be there.
You're the magic I need every second of life.
Daily my soul craves the warmth of your passion.
Though your smile alone laundry crystal clean my sadness,
I wonder sometimes about your effect on me.
There must be some secret ingredient in your sweetness.
Something that enhances the excitement of your touch.
How else could I miss it so much?
How else do I explain why the simple moments,
In your absence sometimes feels like years.
I long for your kisses and hugs.
To cure my sickness for you're my only drug.

This Ain't No Joke

Ghettos, Hatred and Racism!
They would be the smoke in my winds if I ruled the world.
I would fill it with lots of dreams and wishes.
Where things come true.
Where I get things I've been missin'.
Things like you!
My thirsty soul would devour your hugs and kisses.
Drink life from your fountain like the earth swallow raindrops.
Until the softness of your whisper tells me to stop.
There would be no sadness, no lonely times.
All words spoken from man would be whispers of something kind.
Spring and Summer would be the only seasons.
For life would be all about pleasin'.
We would have a super super large village.
Filled with lots of me's and lots of you's.
In the heat of the moment our soul would simply feast.
You would be my beauty.
I would be your beast.
Night would be like day.
Rainbows would kiss blue skies.
Day would be like night.
The Dawn would twinkle with starlight.
Our galaxy would ring like church bells with laughter.
It would be a magical wonderland.
Even moments of disaster would have a happily ever after.
So I hope you really understand,
Why you should elect me to be your man.
I really need your vote!
Because this really ain't no joke.

On Your Leash

If the world could listen in on my dreams and wishes.
Many would simply call me a fool.
But I'd simply say oh well it's all cool.
Because each time I think about how delicious you taste.
I bow my head like it's dinnertime and silently I say grace.
I kid you not to spend one night with you.
I'd bargain with my freedom, even my soul.
For it would be my private forever, my accomplished goal.
I can't really say how the night would go.
Though in a heated rush I'd be on you like a giant lazard.
Lickin' and kissin' you from head to toe.
The moment would be beautiful I'm sure.
It would be something like midnight skies.
Though the excursion would be like the 4th of July.
It would be full of fireworks.
Each time you feel my lips tattoo a hundred hungry kisses.
On the inner parts of your thighs.
Without doubt it'll be a night to remember.
Experiencing a summertime in the middle of December.
I'd be bitin' on your booty and suckin on your boobs so good.
Your moans would be like breathless love songs.
The way I'd be your freak!
It would be simply impossible for you to speak.
you'd swear one night with me got stretched into a week.
Two bodies sweatin in the dark desperate for the moment to last.
I could never get enough of you.
You like yum, yum, yum! I mean even if you slipped and fell in The mud.
You'd still be sweeter than a chocolate cupcake to me.
Even now I can taste you. Finger lickin good, yes!
But you're better than fried chicken.
WOW! I'd love to be the dog on your leash.

When Love Came from the Dark

Jumpin up on your bed lickin all over you,
Really would be a treat.
You better watch out!

The Peace Within My Soul

When I'm alone.
When I'm feeling lost in this world.
I say a prayer each night.
As I gaze upon the sky to wish upon a shooting star.
I unleash my imagination.
I allow my spirits to soar throughout the universe.
In search of something truly worthy of my love.
You my dear like keys to a castle.
Each night You unlock the doors to my heart.
You're the magic that erases my darkness.
I can feel your warmth as you walk into my dreams.
Bringing light, hope and understanding to what it means.
To have an Angel on my team.
You're the Dawn of my twilight.
The hostess that welcomes my gentle breeze.
You're the sunrise of my midnight.
For you're the peace within my soul each morning.
At the end of all my dreams.

Never the Reason

Lost! Hunted!
Captured and placed on Devil's Island.
Now surrounded by the evils of a dark lagoon
Amongst many is where I now live.
Where the fruits of yesterday though plentiful no one give.
Flames that burned at the end of my tunnel seemed extinguished.
Caged in darkness I struggle with each foot fall. I hear ghostly sounds from trumpets of sadness.
They echo throughout the hollow of my soul.
In the distance frightening voices booms, my heart quivers.
Perhaps an enraged King dispensing punishment for misdeeds.
My imagination spreads its wings.
Its search is endless like winds upon forsaken lands.
But desperate for warmth it returns to your world.
To bathe in the moments spent in your embrace.
An extraordinary treasure no doubt.
For you are the diamonds and pearls within my heart.
The girl that arrest all of my thoughts.
You're the light that dissipates my dark.
I swear! Distance will never be the reason we're apart.

Sounds Sort of Silly

The sparkle in your eyes.
Your touch, the closeness of you.
Lifts the weight of the world from my heart.
Its like a life line to a slave.
It's a freedom that makes you feel so alive.
The same as your hugs, your kisses and your smile.
It's a new beginning with each encounter.
I feel as though I've been given a brand new start.
As if the Heavens of sudden snatched me from the dark.
The soft of your whisper creates a peace within my soul
A freshness with an intoxicating warmth.
Perhaps wishful but the moment I feel suspended in time.
I feel a happiness that spins me out of control.
Though magnified is my thanks for the Lord's kindness.
To him in a world with a heart free of pain.
Where nights are filled with many good dreams.
Often I awake screaming out your name.
Many times helplessly dialing your number without a choice.
Fingers crossed hoping to hear the sweetness of your voice.
It all sounds sort of silly!
But nothing is life without you.

Merry Christmas from the Home of my Heart

The season to jolly is upon us again.
I cannot escape the precious feelings,
I have for you, my family and friends.
So in the Home of my Heart.
I will decorate a beautiful tree.
Hang lots of stockings with gifts for each of thee.
As the laughter of children,
Adults alike fill the air. We will all join hands.
Sing some of those old Christmas carols.
I will crave Grandma's turkey guided by Grandpa's advice.
We will once again share golden moments with the blessings of Christ.
So please remember as long as we're apart.
That forever is your place in the Home of My Heart.

On this Earth for Sure

My imagination soars throughout the universe.
Forever scouting for ways to more effectively pronounce,
To delineate clearly the depths of my appreciation.
To make perfectly clear the heights of my thanks.
As it is of great importance in this lifetime.
For the door of your heart to feel the knock of mine.
Should the Heavens or Hell call upon my name.
Therewith a decree compelling my departure from Mother Earth.
I pray you know to my soul how much you were worth.
How many times my spirits sought to embrace you.
For all the little big things.
For the many ways you used your love to assuage my pains.
I am truly very grateful and thankful, too.
To have been blessed to be a part of you.
It's been wonderful and should I be denied another breath.
I will rest knowing I had a dream come true.
I question not the Lord's way though I do often wonder.
How I ever deserved a gift as precious as you.
Whatever the Lord's reason,
Just know in the many ways you've touched my life.
It's been like Christmas in all four seasons.
I wish often I had been endowed with wisdom and charm,
Magic words that give the comfort of being in loving arms.
But no matter what Gypsies with crystal balls may predict.
There's a love for you on this earth for sure.
That will never quit.

An Angel

A daring excursion.
Something exotic with you would super size my joy.
Something in the midst of a wilderness by a lake.
Somewhere near a bay where I can be a boy.
Building sand castles under sunny blue skies.
Just me with you.
So I can be bad so I can undress you.
So I can slip you out of your little secrets.
Lie beneath the heavens and count the stars.
For each mist, like a kiss would caress your body.
Only the glamor of moonlight would witness our romance.
We would privately warm the chill of twilight.
Two bodies slipping n' sliding against each other Love dancing!
Splashing salty sweet kisses upon
kisses Like raindrops on window panes.
Exhaustion would find twinkling starlight crawling upon us.
Your closeness, the heat of your passion dissipates my pains.
I find relief from worry.
I find courage to confront my fears.
I find an end to my search for peace.
In you!
I find an Angel.

When we Met!

Your touch.
The warmth of your embrace enchanted me.
I was transfixed.
Immobilized by the scent of your romance.
My heart drummed the beat of Romeo.
As we danced you were my Juliet.
I felt princely.
I felt I had found the one girl.
Whose foot fit the glass slipper.
For your passion consumed me like quiet engulfs the night.
Silently I watched peace befall you as you swirled around.
I watch your eyes twinkle like midnight stars.
I watched the moon spotlight its applause across the land.
I was wide awake.
Still I knew it was just a dream.
It had to be, for your appearance was like a beautiful fairytale.
You were extraordinary in the midst of sadness.
Your presence permeated the air with a fresh happiness.
I swear! During the winter season the world blossomed with joy.
It was a wonder! Perhaps equated to many reasons,
That explains how rainbows decorate the sky in the midst of a storm.
My soul screamed.
I confessed all my sins.
I entreated our Lord to help me hold onto my dream.
For your kiss was upon my lips.
Though strong! It frightens me to envision us being apart.
In earnest I would not survive your break within my heart.
But live or die forever is the time it shall be a good bet,
Should you wager I'm forever happy that we met.
Each moment! Each hug!
Each kiss!

The years with you have been a special occasion to me. So come close! Let my heart continue to talk to your heart. Together let's consider the wondrous works of God. How two seeds grew to be one tree.
Because it certainly fills me with much pleasure, To wish you a Happy Anniversary!

I Reach for You

It's not just in a dream.
But in all my fantasies, too. I reach for you.
In the wake of midnight when the stars shine.
Also when waltzing across the land.
You witness the moonlight painting kisses,
Upon your windowpane, I'm there, too.
You're biggest fan cheering and rooting for you.
The Dawn! The Sunrise can both confirm my admiration.
The Birds and others watching over you,
Are all a part of a huge congregation awaiting your coming.
Common is our wish like wide eyed children on Christmas.
Awaiting the coming of a jingle bell.
You replenish many lives with happiness.
Strange! may be your effect on me.
Many may say it's more insane.
The way I search for your twinkle twinkle.
In the midst of a constellation where millions mingle.
But of my fire you're forever the flame.
So understand why.
I continue to scream your name.
Many are the ways I reach for you.

Happy Mother's Day

In you! I find a fun life.
The real American dream.
The essence of the pursuit of happiness.
I witness a hundred or more reasons why I love you.
Every time you smile.
Every time my thoughts land on you.
Every time I look at you.
I witness why sunshine touches my soul even in the dark.
It's ecstasy!
An encore of events romances my memories.
I experience a happiness that makes my soul scream.
As if I'm a fish flopping around on dry land.
And you're my rivers and streams.
My sanity, My peace.
The nutrients that keep me strong.
The reason I'm never weak
Because of you I live a happy camper
A spirited gentle man day n' night giving thanks to our Lord.
For touching me with the rays of his light. I'm grateful.
For blessing me with you.
I'm forever thankful.

A Woman's Love

I sit in silence.
The eyes of my soul stare at your picture.
It's really soothing.
It's like being granted three magic wishes.
It makes me feel really close to you.
So close the dreams in my heart come true.
It diminishes the cost of the many things I've lost.
Though still unlike a Magician,
I pull not from my hat a beautiful dove.
For I crave only the arms of my woman's love.
It's what I really miss.
It's something I'll never again ever risk.
I'm simply so thankful,
I have your picture to help me through this.
To lend me wisdom that truly helps me understand.
The value of a simple gift from Heaven sent to a simple man.
One that opens my eyes to a much needed knowledge.
To something special like the stars that twinkle high above.
For from there too came,
The warmth of a Woman's Love.

Candy I Miss (Remix)

Life is truly a wonderful gift.
It's simply beautiful like diamonds and pearls.
We enjoy the moment as forever ties.
A red ribbon around our hearts.
We briskly act like little girls and boys.
Joy! You feel cascading over and down your soul.
For love like mountain spring water drowns your sorrow.
It erases all plans and thoughts of a tomorrow.
As the seconds and minutes forges into a happy hour.
Where my wishful heart entreats the Lord.
To immortalize the moment to make distance on its journey.
To change its end to a new beginning.
To let our hearts and souls keep on winning.
For you are to me what candy is to a child.
You're a sweet taste everything I miss.
The reason the dangers of life are worth the risk.
Death could not erase the memory of you.
You're the total recipe to my happiness.
You're the Candy I miss.

Black Woman

Forever the love of my world.
My candy, the sweet taste I crave.
Your skin is so rich and smooth.
Like the minerals of the earth man use for fuel.
Though much greater in value than diamonds and gold.
For your beauty, indeed is such.
It impresses both the young and the old.
To only the paradise of heaven do it compare.
I swear if ever my foot falls found forever.
Your sweetness still I would not share.
Label me selfish if you must.
In truth it's simply because I really care.
So although many the miles that hold us apart.
I celebrate our anniversary once again.
For the memories of you still erase my dark.
Each time I gaze upon the picture of you still tattooed across my heart. Many probably perhaps label me strange.
Though sometimes even I try to analyze what it all means
Especially each time I experience the magical way.
You still make my heart and spirits scream.
So from my heart to your heart happy anniversary.
I hope all this means we're still a team.

Jingle Bells! Jingle Bells!

Ho! ho! ho! like thunder across the sky.
Boomed a loud voice.
Awakening thousands and thousands of sleepy eyes.
They were fascinated to witness.
The Beauty of a Sleigh pulled by prancing reindeers.
Their leader's nose aglow as they danced upon the air.
Bravely throughout the quiet of the night they glided with the wind. Forging ahead in a tunnel of starlight.
Bearing many gifts they searched for the first chimney.
Twas the night before christmas.
Their job must be done before dawn.
So as the Big Man in red with the great white beard cracked his whip,
They voyaged through an ocean of space like a giant starship
They stepped in harmony like a mighty army.
To assure the parents of each child.
They would on Christmas find reason to smile.
But of my request I need for all to know.
Before they go I need for Santa to hit the ghetto.
So that on planet earth the whole universe will know.
That all went well.
When they hear those Jingle Bells.

Happy Valentine's Day

Truly the greatest.
Is not just description for you
A simple man I am,
Still you find reason to gift me with your embrace.
Some may question your taste, but I appreciate you.
For no matter how anachronistic the world may see my style.
You make me feel like it's the latest with just your smile.
Our encounters make my heart jump up and down.
The way you cheer me on for every little thing.
Simply means so much to me.
Often I'm actually dazed because of a mighty blood rush.
But while many may think it's strange,
I just hope you know.
I love the way your hugs and kisses assuage my pains.
You've always been more than kind.
In dark moments as well as the good times.
So please know it is indeed a great honor.
To have you as my valentine.

Tears Tears

You make me cry.
My eyes fill with tears.
Each time the King of Pleasure allows me,
To wish you another Happy New Year.
To wish you another Happy Valentine's Day.
To wish you another Happy Birthday.
To watch with you the night sky,
As it explodes in rainbow splendor on Independent Day.
To give thanks with you in November.
To embrace you with another Merry Christmas in December.
But most of all,
To thank you for all the love you give to me.
For the many little things you do to ensure my heart's ecstasy.
I'm simply thankful for everything.
For every day with you is a Happy Anniversary.
So I hope you know in the repository of my heart.
There stored shall forever be all those precious facts.
Because I do appreciate the way you've always had my back.
Daily I pray to survive the coming years.
For with you by my side I am sure.
They will continue to fill my eyes with happy tears.

Because You're Special!

When I think of you.
There's a wonder.
There's lots of care.
In my heart I hear your laughter ringing strong.
Something like June wedding church bells.
It's the song I play in moments of despair.
For it brings me lots of joy.
A joy that embraces kids with brand new toys.
My soul and spirits all rejoice.
I feel them jumping up and down even in the dark.
The light of your smile is the beacon showing me the way.
It's all so magical whenever I call on you.
Night or day you appear gentle as a Summer breeze.
There's never a fuss.
I can always feel you close the distance between us.
Your presence! Like the wind rustling autumn leaves.
I can really feel it.
I swear, It's like a breath of fresh air.
It erases my distress.
It reassures me that I am of a special crop.
A crop chosen to be of your harvest.
You're more than special to me.
In my life you play a super part.
When I close my eyes and just think of your kiss.
When I think of the warmth of your embrace.
A sea of jubilance floods my heart.
It's similar to being on another plant in another galaxy.
Where I'm the King and you're the Queen.
Forever is the time you'll be a part of me.
For all of mankind's diamonds and pearls, A King's treasure of silver and gold,
Could never replace the magic touch that revitalizes my soul.

When Love Came from the Dark

Because you're special.

It Comes Much to Slow

Summer's gone, it's Fall, almost Winter.
Though still I feel the warmth of you.
The Autumn leaves remind me of your beauty too.
The bright colors somehow enchant in senses.
In its midst I wonder why am I alone.
I wonder where you might be.
In memory as I stroll down narrow trails.
The scent of love in our wilderness is so prevalent.
The Forest seems to read my thoughts.
As cool winds caress them, trees smile.
Life seems so different as I listen in awe.
To the birds romance our wonderland with love songs.
I crave your company. I close my eyes believing dreams do come true.
As I sit upon the earth at twilight.
I wish for our bodies to be entwined.
Though I invite not the beauty of the twinkling stars.
For I can only extend such an invitation.
To the expiration of the moment that brings tomorrow.
I miss you terribly so.
The Dawn that brings us together comes much too slowly.

Thank You

I once walked in the shadows of despair.
Though with a smile.
I was lonely with a heart in need of repair.
I was a Bad Boy.
My wish was for glamor, riches and worldly things.
I was simply lost.
I now stand in the light of someone who cares.
The focus of my perspective has been properly adjusted.
Thankful I am, for answered has been my prayer.
For good cause I made amends.
I surrendered my soul to a power greater than me.
Thereupon I requested a friend.
Then came you.
In your letters I found lots of laughter and lots of joy.
My life now feels like a miracle. I pleaded and got exactly the therapy
I needed.
The way you brighten the heart of a Bad Boy.
I question not whether you were heaven sent.
I would just like to personally thank you.
For greatly you ease the pains of what I go through.

Happy Valentine's Day My Dear

No one ever lied.
When they said love can be wonderful.
The times when I thought my life was at its end
Your candlelight brightened its path with happiness.
Your love was like magic hands that touched darkness.
Instantly it erased all traces of my sadness.
You restore within my soul things I truly miss.
You give me the things I truly need.
Things I pray for each night when down on my knees.
Things that make complete all of my dreams.
Things that helps a man deeply understand
The value of having an Angel on his team.
You are the center of my plans.
The true essence of what my life means.
Even in the midst of a storm the world shall witness.
Across my sky the bright beauty of your rainbow.
As I stand tall proclaiming the depths of my love.
The depths of my allegiance to you.
You're the vehicle responsible for my safe arrival.
For my deliverance from hell.
No doubt! You're the arrow Cupid used to pierce my heart.
For you give me comfort and peace within all the time.
So understand why it gives me so much pleasure.
To wish you a Happy Valentine.

The Things I See

It's easy to see what you're made of,
You sparkle.
You wear the warmth of a mother's love.
When I look through the window panes of your heart,
I see a little dancing ballerina.
I see a sunny warm romance.
You remind me of a love song that has no words.
Something pure like the chirp chirp melody of the birds.
You're forever full of goodness though much is your mystery.
For how can the twinkle twinkle of starlight make laughter.
I don't really have an answer.
I just know what I hear whenever your eyes meet mine.
Whenever you smile.
Whenever we kiss and you whisper your words.
My heart, my soul and my spirits all experience.
The glamor and splendor of a real paradise.
In many ways you color my world simply beautiful.
You give me a special kind of freedom.
You make me feel like a stallion in your pasture.
Though tamed free to run wild.
I love the comforts of your universe.
In my world you're the jewels of a pirate's treasure.
You're valuable and rich in all your ways.
By my heart...
You're desired and shall be forever sought after.
With each of God's passing days.
What I feel for you.
Some may call it infatuation or maybe even fantasy.
Still I'm thankful for the things I see.

No Sympathy

It's a rough road.
The journey had been difficult at times simply hard.
But through it all I've kept my faith in the Lord.
Daily I do my best constantly paying my dues.
To achieve a taste of happiness in a world that's cruel.
I try to survive the lies.
Words that break hearts and bring big tears to your eyes.
I fought, I've braved many battles.
So I wonder if it's not yet my turn for a sip of victory.
To get an applause from your heart.
I wonder how one smiles in the midst of agony.
My search seeks no sympathy.
My goal, my endeavor is to shine naturally.
Under the lights of your heart.
I seek to be released from the curse of a mighty dark.
I seek to discover the taste of love again.
I seek to freely embrace a friend.
I seek to embrace somebody special.
Somebody that might be able to fill an emptiness.
Somebody with the power to wash away the tracks of sadness.
I'm asking for a chance to live again.
I'm asking that my heart be allowed to dance.
I swear I ask not for sympathy.
I need help from above,
I need somebody to listen.
I just need lots of hugs.

You're the Music in my World

Since you've been gone.
I lie around till the evening comes.
Smoking, drinking stale beer, living something like a bum
The house is untidy, dark and the air is warm.
In its midst I sit wondering what to do.
I struggle to find answers.
It's not so simple when you're feeling blue.
I try to brave the situation, my heart trembles.
Something rips inside it tears at my soul.
It seems my world stops, I simply lose control.
The shakes seize my body from fear of losing you.
Wishful thoughts seem my only hope for a happily ever after.
Not even a can of Popeye's spinach helps.
For me to be strong I need the music of your laughter.
I need something real to hold on to.
I need you to play our favorite song.
The one called "it's not over we're not though".
I need to brisk in the warmth of your smile.
I need you to stop this loneliness from driving me wild.
I toss n' turn each night.
In my sleep I reach for you but you're not there.
I hear my heart when it screams out loud from being scared
Scared of losing you forever.
I cannot deny you treated me well and everything was right.
Though still all I gave you was lots of empty nights.
Foolish out late drinking sometimes sleeping around.
More foolish to not see your dream to have a good man.
Somebody reasonable somebody that would understand.
A second performance with me in your band must seem insane.
I do understand though in all earnest I've changed.
So I'm asking you to wave the magic wand of your heart.

Edward Jordan

I'm asking for another chance.
For you're the music in my world
You're the best thing that's ever touched my life
I pray you understand.
I just wanna be your man.

Enslaved

Mystery enwraps my heart with fear.
I hear strange sounds lurking in the dark.
I hear spirits wishing from familiar sites.
I see no light.
I wonder if I just fell halfway to hell.
Are the flames yet to come?
A heartbreak worse.
No! Can the pain be greater?
My soul whispers silent prayers.
Hoping magic fingers, inflamed candles expel the dark.
For cries pierce the air like chirping birds.
There is no rhythm, there are no words.
There is only a sad song with no name.
Hollow eyes stare with no shame.
As clouds of emotions drip tiny raindrops of pain.
Fear growls in its midst challenging a struggling faith.
Suddenly fatigue transforms thought patterns into confusion.
Common sense becomes the trail of convolution.
Entangled is my foot fall as I envision my demise.
My soul screams for the Dawn for the sunrise.
As a dark twilight ebbs toward its midnight.
Graciously the Knights of Slumber,
Grants me temporary release from discomfort.

Dear Lord

I dreamt I found you.
A touch of warmth opened my eyes.
To my surprise the sunlight had caressed me.
Though there you were too smiling down on me.
Like the stars that make the night so bright.
Astonished! Wonder and joy filled my heart.
Secretly I was terrified.
By the thought of us being once again torn apart.
My soul prayed for something to immortalize the moment.
For just as fish cannot live without water.
And Birds cannot fly without wings,
I fear disaster will eventually be my fate.
Absence being a member of your team.
Even in the moment though my foot may stray.
Daily I harvest the fruits of your love.
For each night I pray.
With each heartbeat I give thanks.

For Love's Sake

I wonder!
In the presence of life can forever end.
Or does death somehow shake its hand.
Perhaps they somehow simply become friends.
Something like ashes and dust.
When blown by the wind to cleanse a curse.
Before their inevitable return to Mother Earth.
By the measure of man's society,
Is not forever the twin sister of immortality.
I wonder will my foot fall end,
Before the artist of life's yesterday paints a picture
A picture contemporary minds can understand.
My absence amongst men is not by my design.
It's difficult to explain as there stands great risk.
A storm may overshadow a land of sunshine.
Plus! Point the finger wise I believe not.
Though great my sufferance it is with sincere hope,
I'm able to plant another foot fall in the soils of hard times.
For strengthen, I am gaining new knowledge.
By the Wisdom of blaming no one for anything.
By forgiving others for everything.
For Love's Sake!
I pray! My deeds will suffice to earn passage into paradise.

When I'm Alone

Many times my thoughts run wild.
Scanning the globe and searching the universe.
Wishing! Hoping to encounter someone special.
Someone with a heart with spirits that sparkle brightly
That twinkle like midnight stars.
I think about building sand castles, too.
Something like those on mountain tops built by the wind gods.
I wonder if there's someone on this planet.
That would enjoy listening to the ocean waves with me.
Someone to witness the beauty of their roll n' tumble.
To witness the way they playfully splash salty kisses.
Upon the faces of lonely rocks.
I would love to share myself with someone.
Especially in the midst of such splendiferous midnight moments.
Where life is so pure silence rings with laughter.
I crave a sip of those magic moments.
Filled with the roasted taste of your exotic passion.
My heart, spirits and soul salivates with wonder.
For I long to quiet the storm of your body's thunder.
Many the moments I entreat our Lord.
Asking will I ever be discovered will you find me.
Will you rescue me from this prison of doom so seemingly my end.
For my dreams my fantasies seem my only friend.
The Wake of Dawn,
Where the harmony of birds was once alluring, resurrect only grieve.
Evincing tracks from a journey still smoldering in madness.
Still I thirst for a mere sip of you.
A drop of your rain would wash me complete with peace.
For like logs in a chimney birth beautiful flames,
Thoughts of: you keep me Superman strong.
When I'm alone.

World to Me

We've been together a long time.
Had lots of fun pillow fights full of laughter.
I remember times after a night of making love.
Waking up at Dawn in each other's arms was fun, too.
It was fun walking hand n' hand giving strength to each other.
When times were hard, always giving thanks together.
I remember praying together
But occasionally, I know you experienced moments of misery.
Times when your precious little heart would blossom.
Blossom with joy like flowers in Springtime.
Instead of trying to understand what it means.
Foolishly I brought winter showers down on your dreams.
It was wrong, I know.
It's something I make no excuses for.
I just somewhat desperately need for you to know.
Although I cannot claim a reputation for being an educated man.
I am smart enough to see that amongst precious stones.
You're a diamond of the highest class.
Dearly I crave forgiveness for my sins.
To have treated a gift from the heavens like glass.
I pray you understand no matter how things seem.
I'm not trying to lose you.
You're everything that's ever been good to me.
I swear! You're the star of my show.
You play the leading role in all my dreams and fantasies.
In a life without you, ship wrecked my heart would be.
Yes! Although I'm a man of pride to keep you,
I don't mind saying please.
For truly you do mean the world to me.

Your Superman

It's Thursday morning.
Just two more days before the weekend.
Two days before I can open my eyes and feel alive.
Just two days before I can shed these old clothes.
And jump into my new disguise.
I've been working hard all week long.
Nights! I've been on my knees praying to the Lord.
Asking him to give me strength.
Asking him to keep me strong.
To help me survive the feelings in my soul.
Feelings slowly killing me from being alone.
Feelings that constantly keep me thinking.
Thinking about the way you look with tight clothes on.
Thinking about how easy it would be for you.
To turn this old house into a super happy home.
Because each night I close my eyes to fall asleep.
Somehow into my mind into my soul you seem to creep.
Crystal clear is a vision of you shaking your body.
Under neon lights having lots of fun getting your bogey on
Sometimes I feel as though I'm about to go insane.
So excited from watching the way you move
But I don't need no doctor
Because you're the panacea to all my pains.
I swear the way you put me in the groove.
Turns little embers of joy into raging flames.
The way you smile so sweetly makes me appreciate life.
It makes me appreciate everything the Lord gave to me.
And the closer you come drains my soul of all its misery.
That's why I need you to clearly understand.
When you put on your disguise if you wanna be Lois Lane.
I'll be your Superman!

When Love Came from the Dark

I may not be able to leap over tall buildings.
But when it comes to being a man to you.
I won't quit till the job is done.

Thinking of You

I remember you well.
Honey was the taste of your kiss.
In many ways you were just simply sweet.
Never did the starlight wonder shimmering within your gaze.
Fail to fill my cup with delight.
You were always refreshing like rainfalls in the night.
The puddles of sadness in my soul.
You changed into rivers and streams of happiness.
I can still feel the enchantment you pour into my heart
I can still feel the way you could ignite my desires into flames.
The warmth of your touch I still feel like embers in my soul.
Even in the distance they still make my heart quiver.
They still make me reach you in my sleep.
Moments with you were a lifetime of fun.
They were magical as if a spell had been casted.
I swear each time you smiled,
Dawn appeared at midnight with a sunrise.
Your laughter filled the air like a beautiful symphony.
You always played my favorite songs.
Perhaps silly of me, but I would welcome my demise.
To ensure residence in your paradise.
For nothing else would matter so long as we're together.

Thinking of You (Part II)

Sometimes the way I feel.
The way I find myself thinking frightens me.
It actually makes me tremble.
For diseased I am.
I live in a soul infested with sin.
So how can there possibly exist just reason.
To bestow upon me such a gift as you.
I pray constantly to the cosmic forces up above.
For the wisdom to discern love.
Though I dare not challenge Heaven's decree.
I'm just overwhelmed at being deemed worthy of such a prize.
Each moment being a part of you has excited me.
You have been a magic wand to my life.
In the coldest of winter moments and hard times.
You somehow brightened my spirits and filled me with warmth.
Even when I acted dumb you were kind.
I swear! I'd challenged a dark sea for you.
To ensure the love within your heart.
I'd exchange my happiness for misery.
Because you alone,
Are the sources of energy keeping me strong?

Broken Wings Broken Dreams

Nake I stood.
I waited to be showered with sunshine.
But the lights dimmed as the Dawn closed its eyes.
Cold winds blew!
Clouds shivered like a runaway child.
Life no longer kissed.
Rainbows no longer smiled.
Someone hit the wrong switch and suddenly the world grew dark.
Fear festered within my soul and my spirits trembled.
Though powerless to weary to forge another step.
I wept! Praying it was but a bad dream.
As the dagger of reality plunged into my heart.
I was cripped by a binding force of pain.
My knees hugged the earth as I entreated the Lord.
Please make for me to lie down in green pastures.
I confess my sins.
Please mend my broken wings.
Please nourish my broken dreams.
Thanks be to you in abundance for the gift of life.
I ask that you make me a member of your team.

Never Without

Memories of all seasons.
Fall, Winter, Spring and those Summer nights.
We touched, hugged and kissed with our bodies bare.
As solemn promises of everlasting love filled the air.
Under the cover of hope we embraced each other tight.
Heart to heart we vowed before christ.
To sacrifice to make the moment last
Now though the years have come and passed.
Still resonating within my soul,
I find the soft melody from each time you laughed.
The forces in the universe are certainly a mystery.
For never did I ever believe.
Anything on planet earth could tame the beast in me.
Never have I ever known of a beauty that could surpass.
The splendor, the glamor of a sunset caressing autumn leaves.
Until I saw you smile.
Until I witnessed a beautiful sashay as you moved about.
A priceless picture no doubt.
A treasured memory.
I chance not, trying to live without.

Could it be Magic

A million in one you are.
Even when life seems impossible and rough.
You prove to be a total package of good stuff.
You fulfill my fantasies.
You make dreams come true.
Your presence magically dissipates my pains.
In each moment you somehow enhance my joy.
Yes! You are a blessing.
But why me?
Often plagues me with wonder.
Especially when doubt captures and cages my confidence.
More so when I hear thoughts from the dark.
They sometimes flirt and succeed in seducing my heart.
The way you smile sometimes fills me with fright.
The fear opens the floodgates of my eyes.
It brings a downpour of tears like waterfalls.
I entreat the Lord.
To not let there be an end to such a good dream.
I implore him to immortalize my happy ever after.
Then like magic! The lights of your love rescues me from my captor.
I feel it spin me around.
I feel us waltzing across a stage together.
In the midst of splendor befitting a beauty pageant.
So I ask 'Could it be Magic'.
My wonder continues to knock, though question not, do I Your choice.

For you are the total substance of my merriment
To say the least It is within you I find my peace.

Thinking of You (Part III)

To be a part of you is to be blessed.
For you're like a constellation of stars.
You're simply beautiful.
You're greater than my prayers.
That asks to show all children someone cared.
You're even greater than my wishes.
That asked for the world and everything delicious.
In lots of ways you're bigger than my dreams.
Because in you I find everything that happiness means.
It's miraculous the way your love restores my hopes.
Especially in the midst of life's battles.
The way you refuse to allow doubt to overshadow our sunset.
Our Union with each minute and hour finds me grateful.
Your smiles, your kisses and kind deeds leaves me thankful.
You're the reason my soul is peaceful.

Happy Valentine's Day

We give thanks to Cupid.
For piercing hearts with that little arrow.
Granting wishes!
Answering prayers, making dreams come true.
Because of such an embrace from a heart's conquest.
Quence the soul's thirst with a rain cloud of happiness.
The celebration may come only once a year.
But with the moments in life I've spent with you.
I swear my heart has cried many happy tears.
Even in the midst of dark sunshine filled my hours,
It gave me strength to flap my wings.
Like a butterfly that romances the flowers.
I feel the spirit of you decorate the window panes of my heart.
That's why during your absence I thirst for your passion.
The world may think I'm a little crazy. But to me you're really like a special occasion.
Thoughts of you alone leave my soul festive.
Full of bliss all the time.
That's why you're truly my valentine.

Touched by Angel

You germinate my spirits with a pristine goodness.
That which you give to my heart so generously.
Shall forever be to my soul
Like the stars in your sky, a very special part.
The richness of your smile transforms geriatrics.
You make advanced years seem so young.
You tame the beast within that often runs wild.
Somehow the quality of your nature of your charms.
Though strong can make even a grown man seek safe haven in your arms.
You're the reason my world changed.
The reason I'm happy.
Your kiss, the gentleness of your touch diminish my pains.
My appreciation is simply ineffable.
So in small words I can only say thanks.
For the sacrifice of your wings to inhabit the earth.
Solely to free me of a wicked curse.
In this life I believe not in fairy tales.
But I do believe there is Heaven and Hell.
So daily, never am I in too much of a rush.
To count my blessings.
For by an Angel I truly believe I've been touched.

Please Mend! Please Make Strong Again

Often I wonder.
Why broken hearts befriend loneliness.
The lights of brightness.
Are the only antidotes.
Powerful enough to eradicate such darkness.
It's like cancer.
Maybe worse than a combination of two diseases.
It's somewhat like the Dark Prince.
The Will of your soul.
Ultimately it seeks to control. It feeds on happiness.
Like Lice,
It leaves the kitchen of your life in a mess.
Day 'n Night, It'll rob you of all your treasure.
Deny you all that gives you pleasure.
The candle lights that you hold dear.
Becomes extinguished by the dark of bitter years.
As the pearly white color of your eyes grows red from salty tears.
The experience of wisdom starts to elude you.
Each step of your journey starts to feel like the end.
Alcohol! hard drug abuse.
Soon becomes your closest friend.
Where romance once blossomed.
Where rhythm once beautified the sounds of your heart beat.
Lives a hollow emptiness.
A deep rooted sadness.
At Dawn! Eclipsed is your sunrise.
Dark inundates your world.
Cold are the warm moments.
Though within your reach stands many people,
You're alone.
There are no familiar faces.

When Love Came from the Dark

Painfully, you witness a couple's embrace.
As they share a kiss.
Yesterday's happiness haunts you all over again.
Its talons tear at your heart.
Like Vultures devouring a carcass.
Your spirits dim.
Tears crawl down the cheeks of your soul.
Like mountain waterfalls.
Finally, you close your eyes.
On your knees you began to whisper
Please mend my Broken Heart.
Please mend! my Soul.
Please make it strong again!

A Happy Camper

I have a story to tell.
I remember when times were rough.
Your smile and the closeness of you brought me through.
Your touch was the magic spy.
You were simply the candlelight that erased my dark
In a kind way you made life clearer.
The peace within my soul was never before nearer.
The way you used your love so skillfully.
You lifted the weight of the world from my heart.
I remember all those moments.
I remember the soft whisper of all your words.
The warmth they gave me was my sunshine.
They were the freshness of my morning dew.
They gave me more strength than a can of Popeye's spinach.
Like a flower in the springtime, I grew.
Many people doubt the veracity of my story.
They may say it just cannot be true.
Because only people in heaven with wings have powers like You.
Though still if I could turn accolades into storm clouds.
I'd spend a lifetime showering you.
I'd fill the days of your life with pure freshness.
You would be the clear sky rainbows hug all the time.
It's no lie, I'm a happy camper because of you.
I'm a strong man again.
So matter what happens upon my final call.
I just hope we're still friends.

The Magic Wand

Shhh, listen.
There's a special song in my heart.
It tells of my life.
It tells of how you play such a special part.
It tells of a candlelight that lives in a cave, too
It tells of how you strolled into my life.
How you so easily dissipated the dark.
The message is clear in the song.
Its transmission is something similar to radio waves.
It rides the wings of the wind into many people's homes.
Some people say the words make no sense.
Though still its effect they cannot resist.
So they just turn up the music and dance.
As if infested with a new found happiness.
For they too crave the taste of your sweetness.
One would almost believe you to be the candy house.
In a world full of Hansels and Grethels.
I swear you make Christmas come even in June.
You love in such a special way.
I celebrate Thanksgiving every day.
I wish I was smart enough to put it into words.
How much I appreciate you.
Because you are of certain, The Magic Wand.
That makes all of my dreams come true.

Thinking of You (Part IV)

I heard a whisper in my dream.
I felt a soft touch caress me.
A beautiful fragrance aroused my senses.
I opened my eyes to see no one
Still I knew you were there.
A brief moment, startled I was.
But the blanket of your love comforted me.
I felt imperious like a King very important
Then something moved and a warm breeze touched my face.
Dawn arrived!
I realized again it was you my thoughts embraced.

Hooked on You

Oh Boy! Here I go again.
Dark clouds may make attempts to obscure your beauty.
But at Dawn you're like the sunrise.
Forever are the times you come shining through.
Lots of eyes gaze upon your splendor.
Its mystery simply invites lots of wonder.
Even the Winds like lovers whisper throughout the night.
They sip from the glass of your soul.
Though spill not your secrets.
You're chosen cherished are even your tears drops.
For like the rain you make blossoms all of life.
You brighten the spirits of birds and mankind alike.
Daily as they prance gallantly to procure your favor.
You're legendary in your own time.
The glamor of your legendary words may not accurately sculpture
Still Wise Men and Soothsayers voice their fables.
They tell of your warmth as well as of your wrath
Even when the Sun closes its eyes.
Twilight issues lots of invitations.
Many abandon the arms of their slumber.
To chance their hearts being bedazzled by nocturnal charms.
They hope to be the recipient of your falling star.
To make their wish upon.
For Dawn brings only another field of hope to harvest.
Where many will labor under your watchful eyes again.
So what should I do?
The whole world is Hooked On You.

International Husbands' Association in Recognition of Outstanding Achievements...
Proudly Presents the 2022 Wife of the Year Award to:

It's all the time.
The colors of the rainbow are so pretty in the sky.
Reminds me of the beauty I find.
Whenever I look into your eyes.
Something magical happens.
When you smile my heart finds refreshment.
Dreams all come true when we touch.
The warmth of a pleasant wonder fills my soul.
When we cuddle, when we kiss, when we hug.
Location matters not when I'm home.
A Halo I've yet to witness.
Your wings I've yet find.
Still of certain I am you are an Angel.
A recipe of goodness.
For never before you had sunshine ever caressed me at midnight.
Your presence is simply a testament.
God has truly touched my life.
So please know... Forever grateful I am.
To have been chosen as the one worthy of loving you.

We Celebrate his Coming

Like the Wise Men that followed a bright shining star,
To find someone special lying in a manger,
We, too, have travelled from afar
To celebrate the coming of a very little young prince.
But though he has yet to appear in a physical sense,
There in the midst of us all sits a very beautiful lady.
A lady wearing a beautiful smile.
It's easy to tell her eyes view the world through tears of joy.
Something like an excited child on Christmas with a bunch of new toys.
No one really knows but there may have been a moment, a time, when she attempted to hide or
disguise a now
evidenced truth.
Happily today amongst many excited and curious adults,
There is a handsome little boy.
Perhaps not yet ready to face the colors of life
As he continues to rest in the comfort of his dark.
Dearly and proudly protected by the love of a mother's heart.
We come bearing gifts in advance of his long awaited arrival.
We breathe the air impatiently as our souls fill with happiness.
We stand anxious to shower him with love, hugs and a super kiss.
For he is the offspring of a mighty King, a gorgeous Queen.
We ask not that he rush to abandon the warmth of his comfort to please our wishful hearts.
We wish only for him to know that in his life,
We welcome the privilege to play such an important part.
As we sip the chilled chablis from our glasses and our Laughter permeates the air .... be not alarmed in any way.
For we are here to celebrate his coming on this very special day.
So from the hearts of all...
I say God bless you Lady Tina.

There will forever be a rainbow painted across your blue sky.
With love from both family and friends ...
We Celebrate His Coming.

You're Beautiful

Every day in life I've seen ugly
Throughout all of my travels I have felt pain.
I see so distanced the things designed by the cosmic forces of the universe to make man happy so far away.
It's as if I were not included in their plan
But when I look at you instead of ugly I see beauty.
Instead of pain I feel so much joy.
I feel like a necessary part of the creator's plan.
Your beauty is warm like the sun rays.
The beauty of you is so nourishing it gives me strength.
Like mother nature gives to trees that stand tall against mighty winds.
I cannot ask for more than what I have in you.
You are a gift from the heavens.
A gift I shall always love and cherish.
Until the good Lord says my time on this planet is through.
Daily I shall always thank you for allowing me to share my life with you. You are beautiful.

Forever Thankful

Many are the moments!
I feel an ease in the midst of my plight.
Sometimes, I feel the warmth of sunshine.
In the midst of stormy nights.
My sleep like that of a child's brings beautiful dreams
Dreams that paint pictures of beautiful smiles.
Thanks to you, I remember many moments we laughed.
Moments that continue giving me reasons to love you.
For never can I deny a thousand times being made the target
The target of so many wonderful treats.
So many times I've been the recipient of your kindness.
So many times your touch made me a stronger man.
How can I not be your number one fan?
How can I not yearn for your heart to feel,
The knock of my love on its door.
Especially when the spirits that are in you,
Performs so many good deeds without keeping score.
I pray for moments to laugh with you to hug you up.
To be within your reach to count the stars together.
For be it sunshine or stormy weather,
I am grateful to be a part of you.
I'm forever thankful for all the things you do.

I am Lost

I appreciate the sunlight of freedom.
But today's life is like living in a foreign land.
Nobody speaks your language.
I move amongst millions of people, yet nobody knows my name.
I feel like a lost stranger.
A stranger who has no direction.
From poverty, the chill of cold nights, from starvation,
I feel like a stranger who has no protection.
Nights are indeed sleepless.
Stress seems to rattle and shake the window panes of my soul,
Like a tree branch does on cold winter stormy nights.
I feel afraid of a life I thought would be a new wonderland.
A life where I would find my own Alice.
Instead, I feel like a caged animal who has been out of its habitat for twenty years,
And now suddenly has been released back into a dark wilderness.
Yesterday's trials and tribulations were few even though I lived in hell.
I was made to be dependent upon another for survival.
Because of this, today my skills to secure the necessities of life are antiquated.
I feel handcapped.
In a world ruled by technology....
I am lost.

17 years in prison awaiting the warmth of a sunrise to caress my face, I still feel a chill.

I Like You

Lots of words can explain why,
How it all came to be but that means writing a book.
So I'll just mention a few of the big reasons.
When I'm sad you make me laugh.
You make me feel whole again.
You make me want a life free of sin.
More, I like the way your heart reaches out to others.
I like your compassion for life.
I like your personality, too
It sort of reminds me of a rain cloud.
Each drop of you refreshes whatever you touch
Special describes you well.
Though I really like all of you is the story my soul tells.
In all earnest I wouldn't be surprised,
If the world was a box of crackerjacks….
To find inside you as the prize.
Because at the party in my heart you're the music.
Me, I just dance to all of your songs.
A Jester, The culprit of a multitude of mistakes.
Still simply because I like you,
I entreat the Lord to enfold you in safe keeping.
Be the reason my heart is happy,
Or the reason it must weep.

I Miss You

I call you wheneverI can.
During the quiet of your morning coffee time.
During your lunch break or at dinner time.
When you answer I simply say amen.
Because it's soothing to hear a voice that cares.
It's therapeutic to possess something to share.
So no matter what you do,
I'll always cherish and praise all of you.
Often I count the letters of your words
For each I thank you twice for being so nice.
Your words fill me with a special warmth.
It feels like something that could erase a curse.
I pray all the time you continue your good work.
I truly value all you're worth.
Honestly I tell no lie.
You're an Angel, a golden prize.
You fill my heart, my soul with a special goodness.
The way you love brings tears to my eyes.
I swear, it's simply impossible to disguise,
The amount of happiness I feel inside.
That's why each day I need for you to understand,
While hearing from you do keep my soul alive,
It's daily I miss you.
You're much much more than a friend
You're special, someone I can really confide in.

I Wish I Didn't have to Miss You

Lots of times in the middle of midnight,
When lonely knocked on the door of heart,
When winter winds rattled my window panes,
Like something creepy in the dark,
I hugged my pillow super tight.
As my soul filled with desperate hope, I prayed.
My thoughts searched for you like a posse searches for fugitives.
Before I was condemned caged like an animal for life,
You were the Angel that gave joy to my life.
You gave a freshness, you gave a warmth,
The way Sun rays give warmth and life to a garden flower.
Your hugs, your kisses, those are things I miss.
At dawn, I remember the moment I would open my eyes,
The closeness of you always felt like a sunrise.
Your presence, your touch would warm the whole of me.
You were my magic.
Today I am lost in the dark awaiting my demise.
But if I had a thousand wishes,
They would all be for something that would bring you back to me.
I adore you, before you I was shipwrecked and lost at sea.
Inside my soul it was hollow there was never a peace.
Lots of guys relish bachelorhood,
But when it comes to other girls life for me seems insane.
I feel cursed, I start calling them all your name.
I know I've done you wrong lots of times.
Especially when it comes to romance.
Indeed, there are consequences for indiscretions.
I have not the right to even pray for another chance.
Still, I wish I didn't have to miss you.
17 years in a prison cell takes its toll on a human soul. Of my life I relived my yesterday.

It's All True

I pray every day.
To find something in my mailbox.
A postcard, a note, anything will do.
A letter from you would be the sunshine that erases my dark.
It would erase my sorrow.
It would be the reason I smile.
The reason I laugh and play all day long tomorrow.
A letter from you would be a super treat.
Like a bag of candy to a kid on Halloween.
My heart would simply brisk with joy.
Only the Rulers of heaven could tell you how much it means.
Nothing else can ever compete with the things you make me feel.
Even the dreams I have of you leaves me confused.
They all seem so real.
I'll probably never know how you work your magic.
I'll just know with each letter,
My life really feels so much better.
You know, like when big tears come into your eyes.
When you win a prize.
It's all really true.
I swear, It's all really because of you.

Loving your Recipe

In so many ways,
You somehow sweeten the bitter taste in my soul.
Even in the chill of a moment.
When you wrap your arms around me you dissipate the cold.
I feel your passion crawling through my veins.
Hallelujah! It makes my heart scream.
On stormy days or when it rains,
It's rays of sunshine I feel because of you.
I feel a comfort that brings me closer to you.
Often I find myself lying awake in the dark.
Devising plans to color a fresh smile upon your heart.
It's strange how just thoughts of you erases my sadness.
How they make me smile and laugh when I reminisce.
But it lets me know for sure,
I would've been the dog chasing your car a long time ago.
Had I known that you were the pursuit of my happiness.
You are a dream come true.
But if you were the candy in my box you wouldn't last.
Because greedy old me is really loving your recipe.
By the way…Does it really taste like chicken?

My Primary

I never believed in nursery rhymes or fairy tales.
I never believed in the stories from poets.
Those the Elders in small villages sit around and tell.
Throughout adolescent years of my life on earth,
For some reason they left me believing I was cursed.
Darkness appeared in many forms.
Adulthood in all earnest I thought would be worse.
I prayed that the fragrance of heaven I would one day smell.
I prayed for something to dissipate the vivid image of hell.
When I met you I had nowhere else to go.
Much to my surprise your presence, your touch, you kiss,
Restored my soul with a mighty strength.
You gave the landlord of my heart a reason to rent,
Property never before occupied.
To a tenant both beautiful and wise.
Forever be the mystery....
Why yesterday did not embrace my demise.
How today I became the winner.
How the heavens found reason to make you my prize.
Grateful I am to all, especially you.
For allowing my primary dream to come true.

My Wish

To have you on my team,
It would be like going from rags to riches.
It would be the essence, the measure of my dreams
It would mean all my wishes were granted.
If you were the Queen of my planet.
My fantasy as a Prince would suddenly materialize.
I would be untouchable and truly have it all.
Being united with the prettiest girl at the ball.
I would truly have been touched by the heavens.
Truly marked and branded a lucky fellow.
For sure being loved by the heart of a real Cinderella.
The wake of dawn would embrace my twilight.
The sunrise would romance my moonlight.
Time would not exist; life would simply be paradisiacal.
There would simply be the whole of my happiness
The scent of springtime that makes a grasshopper leap.
In my life you would be the beauty of autumn's leaves.
Forever bright and colorful
Forever the reason my heart searches for a reason to please.
The same as Mama's favorite dish.
Forever you'll be my only wish.

You're not Alone

So rich, so smooth is an Ebony woman.
The chocolate texture of your anatomy I remember well.
Gracefully, beautiful you are like fine expensive art...
Distance now negates my reach,
But your image remains tattooed across my heart.
Dearly, I miss the taste of your sweetness.
I miss your kiss and savage passion.
Many are the times I've been close to you.
Still you're a magnificent wonder.
So soft and firm is your foot fall.
I greatly admire the depths of your strength.
It speaks much to the richness of your soil.
Where you carefully planted your principles and morals.
Clearly, pledged is your allegiance to the village.
It struggles, but your heart fails not to answer it's call.
In the wake of a moment you sacrifice your soul.
As the silence of your tears speaks to the night.
Until the dawn stirs your mighty spirits.
Where your heart smiles good morning to the world.
For the show must go on.
Life demands another great performance.
But just know you're not alone.

Erase all of my Pains

I sit in the midst of a dark world staring at your picture.
Wondering what your eyes are really telling me.
They shine with mystery.
Still, I can feel a wonderland beauty raining down on my soul.
My heart beats wildly thinking about the promise of your hug
Hoping to be blessed, privileged to sip on the sweetness of your kiss.
I probably don't have the right to hope for the reality of such a dream to come true.
But at this moment...
It's sweet, it's exciting, it's warm and beautiful.
It touches the inner parts of me like chimney fires touch a cold soul.
It's magical, you're the wings to my imagination.
you're the center, the target of my pursuit in all my fantasies.
I would give a King's ransom,
To watch the sunrise in your embrace.
You're beautiful in so many ways.
Your voice is my favorite love song.
It helps me see that you're the light that dissipates my darkness.
You may really think it's crazy but I thirst for your touch.
Though miles away, you somehow feel so close.
Your pictures are like magic wands.
They've got me spinning around n' around.
I may not have the right to say I love you,
But you really make me want too.
Perhaps, it's all just a dream.
If so, please do not let the evils of life awake me.
I may be mentally lost,
Some would say I'm insane.
Still it is you that ease all of my pains.
So thank you for being so kind.

About the Author

Edward Jordan was born in Los Angeles, California in 1951. He was raised in the streets of Compton. Even though crime became his survival, he always felt there was "a music." He describes that rhythm– something he has to this day– as rhythm within his soul that sings to his heart.
In the year of 2005, he was sentenced to serve 60 years to life in prison. Unfortunately believing his demise would be in a prison cell, his prayer was to leave the world with a gift: joy. For all 17 years and 4 months of his incarceration, he wrote poems. His joy and love for humanity was trapped behind bars but never ceased. After being released in July of 2021, he is delivering his gift to all of us in these 257 pages of love.

www.ingramcontent.com/pod-product-compliance
Lightning Source LLC
LaVergne TN
LVHW021803060526
838201LV00058B/3219